omnibus 2010-2011

Our best articles, stories, missives and rants of 2010 and 2011.

Mentisor Omnibus 2010-2011

ISBN: 978-1-105-41716-0

1 Rideau St,
Suite 700,
Ottawa, ON,
Canada
K1N 8S7

+1.877.870.2456

http://www.Mentisor.com
info@Mentisor.com

TABLE OF CONTENTS

Mentisor Omnibus 2010-2011

Welcome

It has been quite the year for Mentisor – as this was the first big/full operating year, and we're still in our start-up stages.

Mentisor is comprised of a group of affiliated consultants, companies and industry professionals working together to provide an exchange and source of knowledge, experience, insight, and commentary on a variety of subjects and fields (while still having a little light-hearted fun along the way).

Most importantly - we pride ourselves that our consultants and contributors are all graduates of the "School of Hard Knocks" - with real experience to back them up, and not just a slew of cool looking certifications and book knowledge.

This publication consolidates some of papers, articles and missives released in our first year (and a bit) of operations, and (depending on how things progress) may be an annual or bi-annual publication.

More can be found on the Mentisor site, and Facebook pages at:

> http://www.Mentisor.com

> http://www.Facebook.com/Mentisor

But Mentisor is more than just "text" and social media.

Even before Mentisor was fully off the ground, we've been running our own internet talk-radio show/podcast called the "Mentisor Soapbox" for nearly two years and can be found on BlogTalkRadio at:

> http://www.BlogTalkRadio.com/Mentisor

Here we tackle a broad variety of subjects, including:

- General Business Operations/Management
- Current Affairs
- Leadership
- The Economy
- Project management & Consulting
- Operational Readiness
  …and others.

I've been told that we range anywhere from sounding like we're having a bar room brawl to an episode of Sesame Street depending on the topic – but we've love to get your feedback and, better yet, come join us by calling into the toll-free number (either on the live show, or leaving us a message on our feedback line).

Much of this has been baby steps for Mentisor; the real work is coming in 2012 and 2013 with our "real" business – which goes beyond just being a source of knowledge and experience – and more into classic consulting services – but with our own unique twist.

More on the future of Mentisor will follow; in the meantime – I leave you to our collective "works" of 2010-and 2011 and invite your feedback or even your own articles and ideas.

Stephen Holton, PMP, CISSP, SSGB, ITIL, CD
President & Principal Consultant

Mentisor Omnibus 2010-2011

Delivering to the Solution vs. Delivering to the Customer

Stephen Holton

Many of us have seen it. The notorious "black box" is dropped into the rack, plugged in, powered up, and once a few pings and system or application checks are completed, the project is declared "delivered" and the team quickly disappears.

Eventually, of course, something goes wrong and in many cases an already overworked support team needs to learn on the fly as they analyze and resolve a problem with a new application or service.

Fortunately many project delivery teams maintain a post-implementation support/warranty period where such events are resolved as a cost to the project, versus using steady-state funding (or internal IT budget) set aside for ongoing operations.

In such cases, specialist teams remain on-call and (perhaps most importantly) funded to assist with these last minute integration and support issues (while providing additional training and knowledge transfer to the support teams in the process).

This is fine until either the funding for the post-implementation support dries up, or management declares the new product to be in "steady-state" or "production" mode.

Often this "transition" decision is based upon various technical and training factors (such as a significantly error free period, or sufficient knowledge transfer from a vendor or key specialist to "Joe" who manages the boxes in the server room).

When problems occur post-implementation, a lack of effective operational readiness and transition to production planning can become a nightmare for Joe, the support teams and the IT organization at large.

Delivering to just the "Solution"

Projects are essentially just the manifestation of the deployment of a "solution" to some customer problem. It must, of course be tangible as well as both resource and time constrained.

The problem, however, is the solution is usually defined in the vacuum of an idealized model, or (if you're particularly lucky) within the overall environment and related systems at the time the "solution" was negotiated and designed.

While this solution often addresses the key architectural and technical specifications necessary to complete the design, build and deploy for the project - it remains predominantly technically focused, and fixated on the point in time the solution was developed.

While your solution may be built in accordance with the specifications, and appears to pass all acceptance tests when plugged in, it has actually only started the first phase of the overall delivery process to the customer.

Delivering to the "Customer"

The "customer" exists in a dynamic environment, with requirements which go beyond the pristine model of any initial solution.

Not only has there been changes since the original solution design which need accommodation (i.e. inter project dependencies, new initiatives, changes to the baseline infrastructure, etc) but the customer's total needs are rarely satisfied with just connecting a product to a socket in the wall.

Ultimately the new product or service being deployed will become part of what ideally is a thriving business, and it sometimes helps to think of it in this "living" context.

Essentially you've not only brought a new puppy home, but now you have the added problem of its care, feeding, watering and cleanup.

Multiple Customers/Consumers

Before you can assess what is required to successfully support the application, you need to identify the customer.

As with most projects and stakeholders, there are many "customers" to whom the solution is actually delivered – often generating supplemental deliverables above what was contained in the original specification/solution.

There are, of course, the ultimate end-users of your solution; but they are just one component in the overall delivery. Key service and support teams also need to be viewed as customers, and must have their requirements analyzed in order to determine what's needed with the delivery of the solution.

For example, Joe and the support team will require manuals and configuration guides; the service desk may require quick reference cards and end-user documentation.

The requirements go beyond just documentation however, as the care and feeding model still applies – interfaces with existing service and delivery support processes and procedures are also required.

The puppy is more than just a "deliverable" to the kids (along with a copy of "Puppies for Dummies"); the sanction and support of other key "stakeholders" within the family is necessary in order to maintain unity – whether it's Mom agreeing to deal with the extra pet hair around the home, or Dad walking Rover while the kids are at swimming lessons after school.

The new "box" delivered to the customer must fit within the overall operational context of the IT and business environment at large, and if it doesn't fit – then either the box or the business/IT support organization needs to change.

Certainly some of these factors may have been considered during the initial design of the solution (i.e. where the box was to be connected and assigning it a network address), but the longer term requirements must also be accommodated. This becomes part of the management of the production or steady-state environment – such as network capacity requirements as the user base grows, or the space and time necessary for backups.

While everyone knew the new puppy needed a dog house, and Dad started to build one as Mom and the kids were getting the new dog, there could be significant problems if someone neglected to mention the puppy the kids settled on was a Great Dane.

But we already have an activation checklist...

Many organizations already have system activation checklists which outline the necessary steps and agreements necessary for installation of a new

system or service – but these are largely technology focused. Transition to production activities, and eventual operational readiness, must take a larger holistic view of how the new solution fits within the overall business and IT environments.

This view should go beyond the initial parameters of the project; an overall product/service lifecycle needs to be considered – from the installation/initiation of the solution, to ongoing maintenance and support (the care and feeding), and to its eventual retirement.

Other business domains are also implicated (i.e. human resources and staffing, training and financial management; questions of what the cost of ownership of this new service will come up, as well as a determination of who owns the burden of those costs, etc).

Viewing the hardware or application as a service that must fit within the overall service framework of the organization is a great start. Working within ITIL's[1] process framework (even if not an ITIL shop) can be an excellent start-point when assessing the overall requirements and impact on the organization.

For example, borrowing from the ITIL processes [2]

Service Support Processes

- Service Desk/Service Request Management
    - Who will support the new box/service?
    - Do the end-users know how to contact Support?
    - Is Support staffed sufficiently to answer calls about the new service?
    - What service requests might they receive, and are there processes/procedures in place to provide for these requests[3]? Who approves them?
    - What are the associated costs, and who bears them (see Financial Management)?.
- Incident & Problem Management
    - What is the end-to-end path for dealing with service outages and systemic faults?
    - Are all parties aware and integrated with appropriate agreements, standards, tools, etc.

- o Is this consistent with support processes for other systems/services? Does it need to be an 'exception'? Have the implications been considered?
- o Are there escalation processes to deal with more urgent situations or excessive delays?
- o Are there knowledge base/materials to assist teams in supporting the new application? Has a process been established to capture lessons learned and solutions to known problems?

- Release and Configuration Management
  - o Have appropriate processes been established to deal with modifications and upgrades to the application or service?
  - o Are they key stakeholders known? Have formal approvers been identified within a change management process for this solution?
  - o Is there a communications process/strategy in place?

Service Delivery Processes

- Service Level Management
  - o What are the customer expectations in terms of service availability and support? Are these formal, contractual commitments?
  - o Can the Service Support processes, procedures, staffing and capacity actually meet these commitments? What are the implications if they are missed?
  - o How are service levels being monitored and reported? Have the key performance indicators been identified?
- Capacity and Availability Management
  - o How are capacity and availability being monitored?
  - o Who is responsible for expansion (or reduction) of the environment/service?
  - o How do availability and outage metrics get integrated into overall

service level and continuity management?

- Continuity Management
  - o Is there a disaster recovery plan in place? Has it been tested?
  - o Are there backups being performed, and have they been properly integrated with other backup and continuity practices in the organization?
  - o How quickly does the customer need data restored? How soon must the service be restored in the event of a total failure?
  - o What is the overall cost/impact of an outage[4]?
- Financial Management
  - o Are the costs of the system known and understood?
  - o Have these costs been incorporated into the annual operations budget, or has a cost-recovery/billing mechanism been put in place now that the product or service has gone live[5]?

Development of your own checklist of transition to production/operational readiness evaluation criteria, customized to the specifics of your organization, will go a long way to facilitate future delivery planning.

One great approach is to look at the formal definition of each of these ITIL services, and then perform a "so what?" devolution/analysis, but this is better left for a future article.

It should also be stated that not all the answers to these questions are going to result in action items for the project team; some go to the core of how operations and services are maintained within the IT organization at large – and become a larger, organizational problem to resolve.

Who's Responsible?

One of the largest points of contention is the responsibility for planning and development of the transition to production deliverables. Does it reside with the steady-state teams required to ultimately operate and support the new service, or with the project team who delivered it?

Candidly, it's a mix of both; however the burden of responsibility should rest with the team introducing the change to the steady-state environment – the project team.

The steady-state teams should be responsible for setting the standards and facilitating the planning for transition. Ultimately they should be serving as gatekeepers into the production environment – ensuring anything newly introduced is ready, and will not destabilize the environment or operations.

If this occurs, acceptance into steady state should be rejected until either the discrepancies are remediated (by the project), or the project team has a plan to mitigate the potential risks (which may even include "acceptance" by the gatekeepers of the steady-state environment).

Conclusion

Delivery merely begins with plugging in the new system or service, and the efforts in planning the overall transition to production and ensuring operational readiness may be comparable in size to those involved in the design of the solution.

One of the hidden costs that often impact an IT organization is failing to recognize the project's commitment to complete this transition process.

Failing to plan is planning to fail, and in the context of operational readiness this failure can haunt the steady state teams throughout the entire operational lifecycle for years to come.

That cute little puppy the kids lost interest in eventually became a full sized dog that is now the whole family's responsibility to care for.

End Notes:

[1] The Information Technology Infrastructure Library (ITIL) is a set of concepts and practices for managing Information Technology (IT) services (ITSM), IT development and IT operations. The names ITIL and IT Infrastructure Library are registered trademarks of the United Kingdom's Office of Government Commerce (OGC). [cited from Wikipedia.org - http://en.wikipedia.org/wiki/Information_Technology_Infrastructure_Library]

[2] Yes, I've taken some liberties by combining several processes and simplifying them in these examples.

[3] Think about password resets, new accesses, termination of access, etc – the list grows pretty quickly from there.

[4] You'll need to know this if you want to prioritize repair efforts when multiple systems go down.

[5] I've seen new systems deployed where someone forgot to advise the finance team and thousands of dollars in revenue were lost before someone finally caught on there were monthly recurring charges to the customer missed with activation of the new service.

Wiki-assault Primer

Fred Parker

Recently, one of the websites that I own and maintain was subjected to an organized, (and I did not realize at the time) reconnaissance-driven and scripted robot-attack, which specifically targeted a particular flavor of Wiki-software.

The mechanics of this attack were, to say the least, fascinating, and a more fortunate part of this scenario (if there can be a fortunate part) was that I was at a place and time where I was actually able to, sort of, let this thing go... that is to say, I watched it evolve, only taking the minimal steps and counter-measures to protect the website at each stage of the attack as it evolved. The content of the Wiki and the few members' personal information (which comprises only of their email addresses that they used to register their Wiki-accounts, on this relatively new "start-up" website), were never in any danger.

The goal of the attack was simple, much like a Forum-spamming attacks that post messages in Forum-threads - to create accounts and post pages that contained links to malware- and virus- server-farms.

What set this apart from anything I have ever seen before was that in the first couple of days - I would have sworn I was chasing after a malcontent with a personal beef against me whom I suspected was using proxy and/or anonymity services to hide his true location and identity. The Visitor Logs did not immediately lead me to the conclusion that there were scripts or robots involved... I had gnawing gut feelings... but I was also "ticked off" at several points by the activities of what turned out to be a phantom.

On the third day, I cursed when I thought the person figured out my sleeping habits when I awoke to find the results of a larger-scale assault than had been seen in the previous days on the Wiki, with dozens of accounts created and pages posted during the overnight... however, as you'll see in my next blog posting, this was just the beginning of the second-wave - after the first wave had finished scouring the web in search of vulnerable wikis.

In the early-stages, to further my clouded judgment, the links being posted in the Wiki were pointing to a "search-page" which, with a few quick searches and verifications of my own, told me that it was a portal to bot-server-farms... so I still took it as an individual trying to tarnish the reputation of the Wiki/website by linking to a known hostile-hotspot... it wasn't linking directly to the hostile servers, it was linking to the link.

I almost became too absorbed with the "personal" attack, that I almost overlooked any potential of it being scripted. I put two "almost" in there on purpose... I always had a sneaking suspicion that something wasn't right...

The pages being posted in the Wiki were eerily "subjective", not in terms of the actual theme of the Wiki itself, but in terms of relating to "me", the owner of the website. The content of the pages being posted on the Wiki in the very early stages were very relatable to me.

Now, to make this all "make sense" to you, the reader - the Wiki is based on an Online Game which is Team-oriented, where I am a well-known member of the Game-site Community, namely because I have started this Wiki. Coincidently, I recently and kind of suddenly moved one of my game-characters from a Team where he had played for quite some time, and this ticked some people off. Forgetting that this is "just" an online game, and noting I have created an offsite-wiki and will soon be opening a kind of social-networking section of the website to help support and expand the wiki-section, there are some people who take this game quite seriously! Thus, the timing of all this was ripe for script-kiddie conspiracy!

Alas, once the flood-gates opened on that third day, it became quite obvious that it was no longer an individual with a gripe, and the pages being posted were no longer strictly relatable to myself. It was now clear that it was an all-out attack on the Wiki... and what do you know, the same day, an email arrived from the Wiki authors, advising to upgrade to the latest stable version of the Wiki-software. Among the listed fixes in the release is an SQL-injection fix - which is what immediately catches my eye, since my Content Management System has Injection Protection and has not "caught" anything during this entire drama... and for all the counter measures I installed on top of the CMS, short of updating the wiki-software, I had even mentioned to a friend at one point that the only way I could see that they were still able to create accounts and post pages by this time was if they were hacking the database!

So, I learned that even though the Wiki-software is installed within the folder structure of my CMS, because it is not a component, module, extension or Plug-in of the CMS, it is not protected by the Tools of the CMS! Neither does it seem to have been FULLY protected by other server-level security software packages that were also installed in efforts to stop the waves of attacks at various stages - they had some blocking effect, but did not prevent the SQL-injections for account and page creations.

Long story short (and the longer story will be coming with full details of the attack, how it started, how it unfolded, who was responsible and how it was stopped from affecting the Wiki... but they're still knocking very hard at the door... so they have not run any robots yet to see who has patched the vulnerabilities), the direct assault on the Wiki is over for now... but maybe not these guys, but someone else will be back sometime down the road.

A Wiki on a website, especially any kind of collaborative or production website, is a must-have now - just like Forums were, and still are, and we all know how Forums have been attacked by these kinds of spamming assaults for a long time now.

Word to the wise, if you are going to have a Wiki on your website, make sure it's well supported... and just like you have Forum-Mods... you NEED your Wiki-Admins, and they need to know not only the day-to-day upkeep tasks, they need to be on top of the day-to-day updates of the Wiki-software itself!

Wiki-assault, Part-do
(yes, it's a French joke)

Fred Parker

Since I posted the first part for this article, and as a result of numerous updates to the Community that uses and updates the Wiki in question, I have been practically inundated with one single question (with another benign, but expected follow-up); why would anyone bother to so ferociously attack a Wiki about an online game? What could they possibly gain from attacking a Wiki with such a small number of members?

The first kind of off-base assumption is that ours was the only Wiki targeted in this attack. The next assumption is mine, and that would be that the people asking the question are also assuming that the attackers had a very singular goal – like harvesting user-information.

So, let me first review what the actual intent of the attack was: to post links to malware- and virus-server-farms.

The goal: that Wiki-viewers would browse to these pages and click these links, thus infecting their machines with whatever flavor of bad-code resided on the server that the particular link pointed to. What that bad-code could or would do is anyone's guess – I would assume that there would be any variety of information-scraping tools, to robots waiting to take your machine over as part of a larger scale attack in the future... who knows? I certainly didn't click any of the links to find out after I researched what the links were pointing to!

Before I detail the events as I promised I would in this follow-up, I wish to re-iterate that my point of this article is to inform anyone who has, or is considering to have a Wiki on their website. During my research of this event, what became evident to me is that this is not going to be the last time I am going to be facing this type of assault, or another from a different angle. As the tag of the article suggests, this attack was achieved through SQL-injection, future attacks will be a surprise, I'm sure. The bottom line is that the hackers, spammers and script-kiddies have realized that Wiki use on Websites is common now, and proper security of those Wikis isn't as common!

Day-1: I awoke one morning and checked the Wiki recent activity as usual, and noticed a new entry for a new page by a new user titled, "Job Opportunities in Canada". I looked at the page, all it had was repetitive links to different job categories from a certain search-engine results page. I checked the details of the search-engine via Google and it wasn't good, it was reputed to be a known source of malware distribution.

As I mentioned in the previous article, in the actual online game – I had recently and suddenly moved a very high-caliber character from a Team, and some people were not happy about me moving the character on such short notice.

Taking the above into account, I assumed it was a malcontent trying to cause some trouble, so I deleted the page and banned the new account, banned the IP from being able to create new accounts. I kept an eye on the Wiki throughout the day, nothing unusual happened. Problem solved, I thought.

Day-2: Woke up to find that overnight, three (3) new accounts and three (3) new pages had been created the overnight. Two (2) pages were "Job" related Page Titles, but now specifying City names in Canada, and the third page was a "find a date" type of Page Title. As with the day before, I simply deleted the pages and banned the accounts. I checked my recent visitors reports, and that is when I was quickly able to determine that "whoever" it was, they were using proxies to create accounts and post new pages... blocking and banning was not going to stop them... if this was an individual, this was going to be a battle of nerves and endurance. No new accounts were created that day.

Day-3: Things got a bit more aggressive this overnight, still only 3-new accounts posting 3-new pages, however there were also two (2) more new accounts created at approximately the same time. I deleted the "spam" pages and banned the accounts that created them, and later in the day, the two other accounts did create "spam" pages, so they were deleted and banned too. I started to suspect a scripted attack, so I installed a CAPTCHA extension to the Wiki. I also found a Blocking Software that blocks most known proxy sources used by spammers and hackers, and spammer-tolerant hosting services worldwide. From the point that I deleted the two other pages and accounts created overnight, there was no other "bad" activity.

Day-4: The flood-gates opened! Overnight, over two-hundred and fifty (250) accounts and dozens and dozens of new pages titled with every imaginable "spam" job/dating/vacation-deals/car-for-sale teaser had been created. Fortunately, none of these entries were tapping into any Category or any other indexing or listing capability of the Wiki, so the only real way that anyone browsing the Wiki would find them would be to look at the "Recent changes" link. This Wiki does not include any Front-Page extension that displays recent additions.

It was obvious now it was a scripted attack.

I immediately advised the Community about the pages and the links, and set about determining how they were bypassing all the security layers that were implemented, both before, and at Day-3 of the attack.

After combing the Logs from the previous five (5) days, I noticed two things that stood out.

- baiduspider+
- Yandex

Both of the robots were bypassing the robots.txt file, and coincidently, both of these robots visited the website immediately preceding the creation of new

accounts and posting of new pages in the Wiki. I won't expand on the details or make any direct accusations, y'know, save myself any potential slander accusation... just Google, you'll find all the info you need, including full sets of primary and alternate IP-addresses you can add to your own block lists if you so desire!

I was still very frustrated though. I am very security conscious, and aside from the Front-end protections I had already, with the addition of CAPTCHA to the Wiki, and the proxy and spam-tolerant host blocking software, I was frantically searching for, installing, testing, getting more frustrated, uninstalling and looking more – and getting nowhere... the number of new (spam) users had climbed to over 750 by this point, and hundreds of (spam) pages had been posted.

When I was in about the 4th or 5th hour of my research on this problem, my email inbox dinged – lo and behold a message arrived from the authors of the Wiki-software I am employing on my website, advising me to upgrade to the latest release for some VERY important fixes. First on the list was an SQL-injection fix – and the "aha" moment was there.

With the problem identified, I was now able to "manage" the situation.

I watched it over the next few days, and while the scripts were still able to sneak in a new account creation by the protections I set in place before I upgraded the Wiki, and an occasional page was posted, I was always able to delete and ban within minutes thanks to an email alert.

The Visitor logs were what I was interested in, and sure enough I got the information I wanted. The suspected agents continued to visit the website just prior to an attack, ignoring robots.txt every time.

Once the Wiki software was upgraded, the scripts continued the attempts to access the site and create accounts for about two (2) weeks.

An interesting footnote is that at that same time, new robots with very exotic names started visiting the website. Trusted website resources usually noted these new spiders to somehow be related, although sometimes the web of links was very long... indicating that perhaps this is part of a well-organized and long-existing "ring" of hacker and spammer script and server sharing resources. What I do know is that the number of Wikis that I found that were exploited by this attack while I was doing my research was phenomenal!

The moral of the story – do not take Wiki-management lightly. To be more specific, website management as a whole needs to be approached with an eye on security, an ear to the ground, and feet on a solid foundation, so to speak.

As more people are approaching me for advice for their existing websites or to create a website for them, the one thing I see and hear is that they all want the coolest and "hottest" technology out there – they want it put together for minimal costs, and they don't want to have to know a lot about keeping it running... where's that "Price is Right" - dun-dun-de-dahh - whaaaaah horns – sound when you need it? (Oh, here it is!)

Look folks, that will maybe work if you want to have a nice little website just for you and your friends, but if you're expecting to have a Website where you want worldwide attention and international traffic open to all countries of the world, AND you want any measurable level of user-interactivity... then be ready, and by be ready I mean be ready to know everything about how your website works, including all Content Management Systems, Third Party Software, Components, Modules, Extensions... failing that... hire a competent Webmaster

Why users need to take a "hands-on" approach to technology

Stephen Holton

> *Funny... another one of those articles written over 10 years ago that, until recently, I thought was completely irrelevant today – but after having worked with a few government entities that were deploying computers and new workflows for the first time – I found myself repeating much of the same mantra as I had with the introduction of new technologies and computers in both the Army and the Railway industries nearly 20 years before.*
>
> *As with all these "older" articles – the fundamental truth remains valid today as it did then.*

Every time I hear someone lament about how their computer couldn't possibly be working correctly, or it is somehow making their life more difficult because "it" should be here to "do that" (whatever the ubiquitous "that" happens to be), I enjoy handing them a hammer and nails and telling them they now have the tools to build their dream home... get to it.

On those rare occasions that I'm not immediately swatted up the side of the head, I'm often told "I can't... I don't know how".

Yes... but you do have the tools in your hand that can "do that".

Users need to clearly understand that computers aren't magic. Likewise, the myth that "technology will make all our lives easier" is one of the biggest lies since "income taxes are only an interim measure to pay for the Great War". There is a balance; and the pivot point is the knowledge, skills and expectations of the user.

The fundamental "truth" that the users need to understand is that the computer is nothing more than just another communications tool... no different from a telephone, television or VCR.

It will not auto-magically perform all the tasks that will move us into a Roddenberry-esk (yes, that's a Star Trek reference) era of only "happy work" and lots of leisure.

Regrettably, just as with programming a VCR, there is a requirement to spend some time learning about the new technology.

Users shouldn't feel that the technology is being thrust upon them however... and that they are in some kind of do-or-die/learn-or-leave environment (unless that really is your corporate culture).

Contrary to other myths, computers have actually replaced very few people. Instead, workflow and business process change.

More often than not, the "personnel savings" that come from implementing these new information systems are quickly eaten up by the requirement for support staff, subject matter experts, or simply the redirecting of the efforts of the old staff away from their manual duties to now focus upon the benefits of the new system.

Efforts wind up being directed towards system validation and ensuring its operation derives the maximum benefit from the investment (engaging in tasks such as data integrity verification, report generation, monitoring, trend analysis, etc.).

Likewise, the velocity or reaction time of the organization changes – to make better use of the information derived from the information technology – thus creating a strategic advantage (one of the reasons why we embraced the technology to begin with).

It is essential that users understand that act of learning and adapting to change rarely puts the operator or the new computer, technology or work-processes at risk (although a good hiccup in the system can be quite aggravating, and perhaps invoke a heart attack in those operators who haven't seen their doctor prior to initiating training).

I still believe that the greater threat comes from not knowing how to operate and leverage the technology, rather than the risk of an aneurysm from using it.

Ever notice how Grandmother seems to have problems using the VCR (we'll ignore the clock part... since most of us can't do that)?

Many of us view the VCR as a pretty basic technology... put in the tape... press play, record, rewind, stop, etc... and it does what we want. Too simple?

It seems simple because we already possess the foundation knowledge required... probably gained through a similar technology that many of us regularly played with as a child... a tape recorder.

The lesson to be learned here?

Technology is changing fast... and its getting harder and harder to keep up.

There will quickly come a point where a novice user no longer possess the critical foundation knowledge/concepts required to adapt to the new operating systems and software (not without a LOT of effort).

That's not to say that it's going to be impossible; but users must be encouraged to make every effort to LEARN NOW! Encourage novice users to keep "black books" of lessons learned... participate in discussion forums and user groups where they can share their insights and ask questions.

Reward/acknowledge those "expert" users who help the others (yes, this can be a double-edged sword... and you need to watch out that these same experts don't get overworked/abused).

All this effort by the users should be thought of as an investment... and as with retirement savings programs, investing at a later time will probably take significantly more capital to achieve the same degree of gain compared to investing just a little bit early on.

While I don't necessarily advocate the use of pressure or scare tactics, users who want to procrastinate and not participate should understand one key lesson:

While almost no one has been replaced by a computer,

many have been replaced by a competent computer user....

Professional Development (post-certification) for PMs

Mentisor Team

> *This is a continuation of the discussions from our Blog Talk radio show – Soapbox #12 where we asked: What are the post-PMP®/ongoing professional development requirements of a Project Manager (PM)?*

This is a continuation of the discussions from our Blog Talk radio show – Soapbox #12 (http://www.blogtalkradio.com/mentisor/2010/11/29/soapbox-12) where we asked:

> *What are the post-PMP®/ongoing professional development requirements of a Project Manager (PM)?*

Now, for the record, we were referring to ongoing professional development activities within an organization or pursued by an individual; we intentionally left formal "advanced" training out of scope of the original discussion – although we revisit it at the end of this article.

Training Areas

Through the discussion that followed, 4 main training/development areas were identified:

- Practical Application Training & Advancement
- Soft Skills & Finesse
- Technical Professional Skills (and Refreshers)
- Lessons Learned

Practical Application Training & Advancement

Revisiting of academic concepts & re-affirming their practical application to project management (especially in cases where they would have been only 'glossed over' during the initial training, due to the complexities associated with integrating multiple domains and concepts).

These could be further categorized along various disciplines (such as the Project Management Knowledge Areas as proposed by the Project Management Institute within their Project Management Body of Knowledge®).

Doing so also creates a framework where you could plan your development curriculum.

Similarly, once the initial "refresher" of the initial concepts and understanding of the practical application of the academic concepts have been completed, the next logical iteration of this kind of training is to then dive deeper into each of the disciplines – and establish a more advanced understanding of their application.

Careful now though; the original scope of the discussion was ongoing professional development training within an organization (for instance, monthly lunch-and-learn workshops hosted within the organization); advanced topics often lead to more advanced formal training – which is in a separate category from the initial 4 presented here.

Soft Skills & Finesse

The hard to quantify, but oh so necessary skills in how to deal with people, hostile or angry customers, presentation, motivation and negotiation, etc.

Often these are the skills and abilities you only get through working with more experienced practitioners as they either deal with unique situations, or coach you through them.

Once again referring to frameworks such as the Project Management Body of Knowledge® you can readily find a proposed breakdown of subject matter knowledge areas/disciplines.

TECHNICAL PROFESSIONAL SKILLS (and REFRESHERS)

Those things that either involve the use of tools, technology, or other techniques to get the job done and are either affected by changes in organization, new tools or things we simply get "rusty" in.

This could be anything from either refreshers or advanced training on scheduling software (like Microsoft Project) – to unique/Web2.0 and social-media concepts such as using private-Twitter accounts for team-based delayed/deferred communications.

Lessons Learned

Lessons learned reviews should be conducted by project stakeholders and their respective management organizations (most notably the PMO and/or project/program management team within the delivery organization) but often these lessons fail to go beyond the report and the immediate groups that it is shared with.

Lessons not shared are never really learned, and therefore lost. Hosting presentations of the most immediately relevant lessons learned to the entire group not only helps ensure that these lessons are passed on, but can also help further develop presentation skills and award Professional Development Units (PDUs) to PMs who are engaged in those sessions.

Additionally, such opportunities are a great addition to a team-building program.

Advanced Formal Training and Development

This area wasn't originally included in our discussions – simply because it's the one that most people immediately think of when it comes to professional development training – and is usually handled through post-graduate training, advanced courses, next-step training, etc. It is not usually within the context of internal (or individual) ongoing training – although we all eventually start thumbing through the catalogs of courses offered by our local training providers.

A discussion on "formal" development training areas/subjects for PMs often tends to be industry specific as well, so it becomes harder to create a standard checklist for all PMs – where the proposed development areas shown above tend to be more generic to all PM disciplines.

That said, there still are some classic standbys that can apply to most situations, including:

- Problem solving and analysis techniques
- Advanced scheduling techniques
- Formal leadership training
- Teambuilding and collaboration techniques

Motivation

Regrettably ongoing professional development for most individuals is ad hoc at best; similarly many organizations have the same approach – and they often squander great opportunities to distribute knowledge and keep the teams refreshed.

Having a framework to assess requirements and build a training curriculum helps, but then that still doesn't address the elephant in the room.

For many PMs, the primary motivation around professional development activities is to avoid losing one's credential and having to rewrite the PMP (or similar qualification) exam again.

While that is certainly good motivation, as is including professional development progress within one's annual assessment in the organization they work, you really can't legislate any sort of passion for one's profession.

The desire to develop one's skills and promote and expand their trade at large requires a passion and enjoyment of what one does that goes well beyond the scope of just the workplace.

Top PM Tools/Templates

Stephen Holton

> *What are the core Project Management tools/templates and processes? I realize we already have a wonderful "body of knowledge", with its 42 processes in 5 process groups and 9 knowledge areas, but I'm really talking about the "core" essentials. What do you need, as a minimum, to "manage" a moderately challenging project?*

Of course the phrase "moderately challenging" opens up a can of worms on its own, so let's just say that I'm thinking of a situation where:

- you have a project that is more than just a trivial/off the back sheet of a piece of scrap paper challenge

- requires a degree of care in planning and execution

- with a small team of fellow professionals (let's say 10-20)

- over a period of a few months

- without necessarily needing a lot of technology and processes to back you up

It's not an easy question... I've been struggling with it for years, as I've attempted to digest various texts down to their essentials, but I think I have my top 10 list (not all of which readily maps to that body of knowledge I was referring to earlier either – although all the pieces do fit in there); more on this later.

Even as I write the article, I continue to struggle with my list – and keep modifying it on the fly.

In any case, if I had to force myself into producing a hierarchical list of tools/techniques and processes, I would propose the following:

1. Project Initiation Document/Charter
2. Project Scope Statement and Traceability/Signoff Register
3. Issues and Action Log
4. Meeting Record Template

5. Risk/Opportunity Register and Continuous Iterative Risk Management (CIRM) Process
6. Change Register/Change Management Process
7. Project Team Worksheet/Communication Plan
8. Schedule/Scheduling Management Process
9. Information Management Plan & Repository
10. .Project Budget/Financial Management Process

Let's examine each of these in more detail...

Project Initiation Document/Charter

Formally launching a project, with a signed buy-in/acceptance from a sponsor and clear authority for the PM to take action is essential to a successful engagement.

Additionally this document should include:

- A description of the problem to be resolved or business objective to be gained (try to avoid providing the "solution" – unless that has already been defined by another pre-project process)

- What would constitute success, or how it would be measured (acceptance criteria anyone?).

- Who is the "sponsor" of the project (usually a business-owner) and key stakeholders responsible for acceptance, usage and (if applicable) post-delivery support of the project deliverables (an often overlooked group).

- Indication of the budget/funding; this is especially important if the project is still in its early development/design stages – where an initial budget is required just for analysis and planning as an overall solution may not yet be selected or mature.

- Initial assignments of team members and/or other resources – especially subject matter experts, technical specialists, end-user contacts, etc. This isn't necessarily the complete team – just the key players that can help the core project team understand the problem.

Ideally there would also be some kind of indication of the span of control and authority of the project manager; ie- can he or she make purchases? Can they engage in the hiring of contractors, etc?

Some of these may be spelled out in subsequent documents and plans, but knowing it at the early stages can help eliminate some confusion and expedite delivery.

Often there are limits on such authority, so the process or at least a key point of contact should be specified (especially if this is an external project manager).

Project Scope Statement and Traceability/Signoff Register

The Project Initiation Document/Charter usually serves as only a preliminary statement of the scope of the project; it provides just a high level overview of the problem to be resolved and possibly some initial deliverables.

Further analysis and definition is generally required – including the possibility of the identification (and ideally acceptance by the sponsor) of supplemental/implied deliverables that they may not have considered when initially defining the project.

The project scope statement should contain:

- An overview of the problem to be solved

- A simplified description of the intended or ideal solution (if known)

- A list of "SMART" (specific, measurable, achievable, realistic/relevant, testable) requirements for the solution (both technical and business)

- A list of "SMART" deliverables/products from the project

- Any relevant specifications, regulations, standardization and/or compliance guidelines

- A list of tests (if known) that will be applied as acceptance criteria on the deliverables from the project (which may, in part, be derived from the specifications and standards indicated above)

The traceability/signoff register is one of those supplemental components most commonly found in a separate tool or template – but in this case, is added to the scope document to provide a means of tying requirements, deliverables, specifications and tests together.

As the deliverables are produced, and validated against the appropriate requirements, standards and (ultimately) tests – signoff is secured from the appropriate customer representative.

Obviously this becomes a living document as a result – which is the intended effect – so that changes cannot take place without considering their impact on all of the elements in the traceability matrix.

It also ensures that nothing gets missed or overlooked from the original scope, as it is no longer document that is only seen and reviewed in early or ending stages of the project.

Issues and Action Log

Short of having the charter/scope document, the next most important tool/template you can have is your Issues/Actions (IA) log.

An issue is any problem for which you do not yet have a resolution for in your plan.

In the early stages of project initiation and planning, when your plan still isn't formalized, the IA log will become your key reference of who is doing what and how you intend to address all those little outstanding items of business.

After your plan has been created, the little problems that creep up and require resolution can be tracked in your IA log until they are either resolved, or you incorporate the solution to that issue as part of your modified plan (often through a change request).

Meeting Record Template

From the initiation of the project right to its closure, like it or not, the primary means of getting people directed towards their tasks, resolving problems and getting guidance is through meetings.

With such an important activity, it would only make sense that recording the outcome of meetings would naturally be crucial to a project manager and his team – but it is amazing as to how many meetings are held, and no formal record of what was decided or who is doing what, is actually created.

There are some simple means to do this – one of which can be found in our recent article on Tips & Tricks: Quick Meeting Minutes at http://tinyurl.com/mentisor-minutes .

There should always be a record of every key decision in the life of a project, and there really is no excuse for keep track at meetings with something as simple as just what the major decisions and action items, by assignee, were.

Risk/Opportunity Register and Continuous Iterative Risk Management (CIRM) Process

Risks are similar to issues in that they are events that may have a damaging impact on your project if not dealt with (or a positive effect, in the case of an opportunity) – but there is no certainty that the event will actually occur.

As a result, you need to decide what to do – either by:

- accepting the situation and choosing to do nothing until it occurs (to take no immediate action is an acceptable choice in some cases);

- taking some pre-emptive action to mitigate and minimize the likelihood of the risk (or expand and exploit an opportunity) – but it takes time, effort and resources and the return on that investment had better outweigh those costs;

- transferring the risk to another team, project, stakeholder, outsourcer, or whatever – but always at some cost to someone – once again raising the issue of return on investment; or

- similar to acceptance – establishing a contingency plan to be executed on the first indications that the risk or opportunity is about to occur (usually done after whatever mitigation/exploitation has been done); this too costs resources – but having a well thought out, understood and approved plan that is ready to go can often offset a larger disaster that you may otherwise need to react to without any preparation.

The problem is many project managers and their teams only pay lip service to risk management, creating a quick list of things that "may go wrong" (and often a vacuous list at that) and then fail to develop any kind of formal response or action plan.

In those cases the risk review is only conducted a few times (or even just once – at the beginning of the project) and often neglected until problems arise.

A proactive stance is critical to effective risk management, and hence the reason why the template is also accompanied with a simple process that outlines the who does what, frequency of reviews, raising new risks to the attention of the project management team, etc.

Change Register/Change Management Process

As military leaders are often fond of stating: "No plan survives contact with the enemy", the same is often true of project plans as they enter the delivery phase. The only thing that remains consistent in life is change itself, and as a result you should to manage it just as you would manage issues and risks.

Key to successful change management is having a register of all the change events that take place within a project (including all those little low-cost/no-cost changes that we often let slip by as they are within our available contingency/budget reserve).

While not all changes may need a formal change request – enough little ones, when grouped together, do – and hence the reason why it is essential to track all change events – both major and minor.

Some form of directive on change management should also exist – even if it's to outline who approves what, and the process for requesting such changes. Even having just a few simple directives in your project charter or plan, coupled with your change register, will go a long way to keeping change effectively control.

You cannot prevent or disallow change; it can be imposed upon you just by virtue of events or authorities outside of your control (including Mother Nature).

You can, however, manage how you deal with those changes – and ensure that decisions made on how to meet change don't live on to haunt you too badly later.

While I'm generally not a big fan of covering my softer body parts with a layer of paper, change management is one of the few exceptions; trust me, and keep good records.

Project Team Worksheet/Communication Plan

It doesn't have to be a major creation, but even something as simple as just a who's who list – names, what they do and how to reach them, will save a lot of time wasted by those trying to track down the right person when needed.

Ideally, and if you have time, you can expand this simple contact sheet to include other great contact/team and communications information such as:

- a standing project conference bridge – for group calls, meetings, etc (including a reservation process if you only have one bridge, and its shared between team members)

- group email accounts/distribution lists – that get the word out to everyone in a team or across the entire project

- social media channels (such as a private Twitter list) that can distribute messages to people's phones or other devices for when they are away from their computer – or in the event you are working in a closed network (but don't send sensitive information in such a case)

- fanout/callout lists – who calls whom in the event of a critical emergency

- a reporting structure if you are in a hierarchical organization (its always nice to know who your boss is, or who can make decisions on their behalf if they are absent)

- customer contacts, key subject matter experts, advisors, vendors, etc

- standing meetings and who should attend

- terms of reference for key roles, and secondary duties

- deliverable assignment or work package assignment matrices – who is doing what today/this week/this month; especially important with large teams or complex initiatives (it doesn't necessarily need to be in a lot of detail; just enough to minimize the amount of "asking around" when someone needs to find out something about another team's work)

Schedule/Scheduling Management Process

You may have thought this would have been closer to the top of the list – and you may be correct in many cases – but I've also seen a lot of projects that were managed "on the fly" with the tools listed above (not idea, but its reality) – so while a schedule is incredibly important, you can live without it for a while if you absolutely have to.

I've also taken the liberty of cheating a little – and I've "assumed" that you cannot readily have a schedule without first developing a clear work breakdown structure (WBS).

For the non-PM types, this is a decomposition analysis of the deliverables in order to derive a set of work packages and, ultimately, activities or tasks which, in turn, form the basis of your schedule.

In truth, the WBS is pretty high up on my list – and if I'm delayed in getting one because my schedule development has been delayed, then I at least start the decomposition of the deliverables into some kind of preliminary WBS in the scope document.

That said, both the WBS and the schedule are living documents – and they should be reviewed regularly with the team.

It's critical to not just look at the schedule and nod and congratulate yourself on your work; you need to go through it in detail with the actual practitioners performing the work and analyze not just what they've accomplished, but to also look ahead and estimate how much additional effort is necessary to complete tasks and whether or not their original estimates were indeed accurate.

This means you need to teach these practitioners who to read your schedule, and to ensure they are ready to provide the input you need for effective management and control.

You not only get a better estimate of where your project stands, but your team really begins to appreciate how all the dependencies fit together, where they can afford to slip if it should be necessary, how to better communicate with you and their peers with respect to those dependencies and, ultimately, to buy into the management of the project as a whole and coalesce as a team.

Of course, education and understanding is key – and you may want to establish a standing process/coordination document that not only explains how you are going to review and manage the schedule, but also key terms, and what information needs to be brought to the schedule reviews so everyone's expectations are being managed.

Don't forget that such reviews are also a great time to periodically perform risk analysis and review trigger events that may initiate the execution of a contingency plan.

Information Management Plan & Repository

Looking at the list above, it should be clear that you could easily be swimming in information – and you really want to avoid having people wandering about asking "where do I find this?"

Some kind of shared information repository is usually essential, coupled with a plan or guidance on how information is to be maintained and distributed (often as an extension to the communication plan outlined earlier).

Some of the considerations are:

- accessibility and availability of data (especially if all your team members are not on the same network, or the information you deal with may be sensitive and therefore always kept in secure or internal systems)

- classification and/or designation of information – as well as "need to know" among your team and other 3rd parties (also don't underestimate the potential value of the aggregate of information from your various sources may represent, especially when interconnected or correlated, which could be of greater value than what the individual pieces represent in isolation)

- integrity issues – as to who can modify information, and whether such efforts are tracked (perhaps even with some kind of version controls); can changes be reversed if necessary?

- duplication, including the threat from having multiple, but slightly varied, copies of the same document – without a clear, definitive (and accurate/up to date) source

You may find that simply having a shared network drive isn't sufficient – and you may need to rely on some kind of collaborative groupware application –

either within your network, or through a 3rd party service provider.

While its often easier to outsource to a 3rd party vendor – remember to keep in mind the potential security risks associated with storing information outside of your immediate control, and think of how embarrassing it could be for your team, your client and their partners should information get into the wrong hands.

Sounds like a great topic for one of your preliminary risk analysis sessions during the early planning stages of your project.

Project Budget/Financial Management Plan

This could just as easily have been at the top of the list – but we've all seen projects that needed to be done, regardless of cost – or costs were managed "on the fly" by senior management or sponsors overseeing the initiative as it was being rolled out.

Less than ideal, a lot of projects are performed this way – and it doesn't minimize the fact that the project team needs to ensure they are being economical and efficient within the delivery of their project.

Tracking of expenses (including efforts) are key, which means you need some kind of guidance that outlines:

- once known/set, what are the budgets for the various components of the project/initiative, including differentiating between various accounts/billing codes (if you use them) and the breakdown between capital vs. operating costs and other relevant details that define your total budget/pool of resources

- who has authority to spend/authorize expenses and procurement; what are the "clip" levels of each approver, before they need to seek higher approval?

- where is the data collected and the frequency of reporting?

- how are efforts tracked and reported (we all know that "time is money" – and that is especially true for the efforts of your team members)

There are many other factors to be included, but these vary dramatically with each organization and the type of project/industry, which means that if

some kind of financial management plan or guidance doesn't already exist with your organization – some serious research and signoff by senior stakeholders and the sponsor is required.

Don't underestimate the impact that poor financial management can have on a project; not just legally for the PM and Sponsor, but also in terms of delivery – since that delivery is dependent upon resources that are ultimately controlled by available finances.

Conclusion

Now I have cheated a little. As I hinted earlier that some of these don't quite fit into the classic definitions of some of these documents; many touch on other documents, processes and knowledge areas than their traditionally defined boundaries – but the objective is to make things lightweight, compact, reusable and serve multiple needs (or have a "cross functional utility" as a marketing guy would say).

The truth is, these form just a skeleton – on which further refinements could be added to flesh out a fuller and more robust methodology.

Most notable in the "missing" pieces that I'd add on right away are:

- **A Formalized Project Plan/Framework.** Oddly enough, few projects rarely get beyond a schedule and a few guidance documents – and generally do not have a really clear or formal project management plan. If you can produce one for a project within your organization/industry however, you will quickly discover that vast sections of it can be re-applied to many of your other projects – and as a result, you can quickly develop a set of standing operating procedures (SOPs) for your organization. The "unique" elements applicable to your specific project can be attached as a separate summary to your standing project plan. This is a highly worthwhile investment in time and effort for any organization engaged in regular projects.

- **A Formalized Project Management Cycle and Development Life-cycle.** The cycle of recurring project management activities used to guide/govern the project teams is not necessarily the same set of activities used to PRODUCE those deliverables by actual developers, specialists or construction workers. The development life-cycle/process is enveloped by the project management one.

Developers/delivery teams are concerned with producing deliverables/product in accordance with the specifications; project management teams are concerned that the developers perform their tasks within the time, cost and quality constraints agreed to with the sponsor (all while mitigating risks, exploiting opportunities and dealing with issues). They are similar, and there are overlaps – and documenting the two cycles as well as their interfaces will go a long way to improving overall success and efficiency. There are lots of development approaches (waterfall, cyclical, Agile, etc) – but most project management tools and techniques are similar. Unfortunately there is a growing myth that you can have a development approach without the benefit of a project methodology – and as a result, only partial governance is exercised – and projects, while technically successful in terms of delivering to specification, are business failures because they arrive to market too late and over budget.

- **A Formalized Testing, Acceptance and Quality Management Processes.** Call this one number 11 from my top 10 above. Testing and acceptance should be planned for from the onset before development begins since everyone will want to be in agreement on how the sponsor/customer will be validating how they have indeed received what they have requested. Similarly, establishing various quality assurance checks throughout the development process and establishing appropriate controls will ensure that they deliverables are correct before they get to the customer. In some cases, having a pre-defined development process (as mentioned above) will also allow for the definition of such processes to be built in automatically within that development lifecycle. In other cases however, it may be necessary to create such quality assurance/control processes are part of your overall project plan – especially when it comes to final testing and acceptance.

- **A Time Tracking/Reporting Tools & Process.** While I indicated that time tracking/reporting is partly involved in both the scheduling and financial management processes above, it doesn't hurt to bring it together into its own clear summary process – easily referred to by all concerned. Having a good time-

tracking/reporting process, ideally tied into your schedule, will help keep your project delivery and costs in track. More often than not, however, the reporting of actual efforts is not readily mapped against the schedule – and some careful analysis (as well as lots of coffee ingestion) will needed to ensure that the project really is on track (a topic leave for another article).

- **Personnel Assessment Process.** Ultimately project management is about leadership, communications and team building – and one of the key tools to help maintain and develop a team is some form of feedback process on how an individual is performing, what they can do to improve, as well as feedback to the employing organization in general on how the individual is developing – with recommendations on future assignments, assessments on the long term potential for the individual and other development needs. See our article on the IPPA at: http://tinyurl.com/mentisor-ippa

Needless to say, the missing/desired supplemental portions to the top 10 listed above could easily warrant a further article in their own right.

All of this, of course, has led to my 10 year struggle developing "small-pm" (a project in its own right) as a light weight, and yet reasonably robust, project management methodology that would lend itself to a broad array of projects, industries and environments.

Version 3 of small-pm is (after several delays) finally targeted for release in early 2012, and will incorporate all of the elements listed above (and more).

It will be posted on the Mentisor and small-PM websites and will be freely available for the public to use.

The Case of the Missing Customer

Frederic Lempereur

> *It was a dark and stormy night my friends. The type of E-mail storm that pushes the mail account to overcapacity in a few minutes.*
>
> *I was sitting in my cube wondering if my earned value would allow me to either purchase my dream car (a Lada with white wall tires) or less of a beating at the next project steering committee.*
>
> *That's when she walked in.*

Over the years I had seen many Project Managers but none that could speak CPI as she could. A single look at her communication plan and any PM would fall off his critical path.

My name; not important as you will see it soon enough (at the bottom of this article).

My job; help Project Mangers when they are confused and need support.

Call it job security for life.

"Can you help" she says; nobody can refuse a beautiful risk plan.

I ask her if she can afford my consulting services. She was told her project was in jeopardy because she had lost sight of her customer and did not understand why.

I asked her to walk me through her project plan in a open kimono approach, "show it all" I told her. She willingly revealed it all, as she confirmed doing:

- Structured project reviews with status, accomplishments, issues, risks and financials.

- Working with the delivery steady state teams to ensure both high quality and on time project activities while providing interim milestone related deliverables as production.

- Engaging the contract manager in order to build customer sign off documents that would have the proper objectives and measurements for the post project life cycle.

- •As a true PMP she had in her weekly activities, team motivation activities to ensure the individuals would remain highly focused.

- Her project plan had obviously included reviews with her up line management team and made sure they were part of the most appropriate communication plan.

- To ensure internal processes and dashboards had the quality required she had been working closely with her Project Control Officer. As a PCO/PM team they had established a true partnership that would allow him to represent her any time she would have had schedule conflicts.

She paused.....and asked me, who is the missing customer?

It was a classic case, one I had seen occur with many PMs, junior and senior ones.

So I asked her one question: who is the end user?

She asked me "What is an end user"?

Project Managers often forget about the end user.

The rigidities imposed by either: project plans, delivery team requirements and/or organizational processes that often make us loose site of the end user who is, in fact, the true customer. Project execution has structured layers that separate us from understanding the end user's needs and their ways of operating.

The IT business office often dissociates itself from the customer, and business organizations often disassociate themselves from IT.

Recent observations show me that IT justifies itself within methodologies that no longer validate customer operations. In reverse, business organisations often operate assuming IT will provide and supply what they need to operate.

The benefits are structured project deliveries. The impacts are customers that do not understand IT project execution and a Project team that does not know how to adapt project plans to customer needs. These new realities become more than obvious when projects become troubled.

What should (or can) be done by the project team is relatively simple; ask questions.

Ask questions that will hopefully trigger further reviews of the solution and execution BUT with an end user focus. Organisational boundaries can easily be taken down with proper communication and willingness.

With a splash of humour above my objective was to present what represents one of the many areas of focus we all, as project managers, need to focus on while the project execution landscape evolves.

The golden years of project management may be behind us; PMOs will now need to bring a refined project management value statement.

There was a time where project management in an IT shop was done by the employee who had shown the most organisational and people skills within a team of IT savvy individuals(also referred to the team lead that had over the years demonstrated success in implementing complex projects). This person usually had followers/supporters in his or her ability to resolve implementation issues, but also had his or her detractors that believed the compromise was a loss of technical skill.

The success of these individuals brought organisations to understand and value them, and value a project methodology that was structured and applied firstly at a team level and then to be implemented at an organizational layer.

This evolution supported Project Management specializations to form and develop unique skills which distanced themselves from the technical spectrum and focused on an ability to communicate and track project evolution.

The usage of, as an example, PMP or PMI in current CVs or in job search activities is a demonstration of this evolution and of this need at the industry level. What could represent the next evolution and how should a Project Manager evolve to maintain a true value add to an organization? Is project execution threatened by the fact it can be described as a set of work products and compartments to be applied under condition X, Y or Z ? Can Project management be offshored to serve a onshore customer ?

Unfortunately I do not have the answer, but I have the suspicion the answer is Yes.

I cannot imagine the evolution of all other areas of IT with some success to an off-shore model to not be applicable to Project Management (or at least some project management).

Let me take you back to my opening story where we are losing sight of "end users" and of their needs. I would think moving project execution to an offshore model would lead us in the same direction. Is it truly a bad evolution?

Probably not; I can imagine some project execution from an offshore outfit to answer very well the needs of projects implementing "black boxes". More and more I am seeing situations where an "appliances" or black boxes, which are standalone solutions, get selected by customers as answering their needs.

Hosting via internet solution falls into this category of IT solution and as all others of the type probably requires little project management.

So where is the need for Project Managers? In my opinion: in their ability to "over deliver".

Over delivery can be achieved by interpreting the principles of a project methodology and applying the elements that are required but more importantly in a manner that distinguishes itself from all others.

Each project should in a sense be creating a new methodology ready to be changed and adjusted for the next project.

In my humble opinion, the moment we as project managers think we have found the way to deliver projects in the most efficient manner is the day we have stopped being Project Managers.

Our worst enemy is stagnation, or a stale project model.

Management is the ability to handle exception or uniqueness – and to ensure it becomes seamless.

Our value proposition is a project management methodology that is unique that relies on the needs of the customer at that moment and of the situation at hand.

Each customer is unique, and each project is unique by definition of being a project. Why do we force a methodology to be applied and to fit? Probably because the methodology has been interpreted as being bigger than the requirements.

So how should a PMO institute a moving target?

The first step is acknowledging and understanding the principles that go along with an ever changing method of project delivery. The templates and base structure must be one that is open and adjustable to each project. The project reviews assume an understanding of each individual initiative and of each individual customer.

An important milestone would be for a PMO to evolve beyond the Red, Yellow & Green dashboard as well as passed the Earned Value, SPI, CPI and other metrics and use them all as important guides - not key measures in themselves.

Each project needs to establish its success criteria probably at the deliverable level. The organization needs to track to that objective. Once a PMO can establish an understanding of the unique objectives a project must have the PMO can then understand the aggregate needs a customer organization would have and hence bring a UNIQUE valued Project Management proposal.

The PMOs that can see the value in delivering to the individual need will then gain the ability to provide highly skilled Project Managers that can be justified in terms of skills and effort levels.

Selling project management in its purest model on projects that require little management as do Black Boxes is becoming a daunting task; but selling Project management skills that are adapted to the needs of the project and the customer gains an easier path to closure.

Project Management is no longer a required service to IT delivery; unless it demonstrates itself as unique, it has reversed itself back to being overhead.

Reaching over the levels of abstraction between project managers, through the PMO and other organizations and process, to the end-users themselves will go a long way to bridging the perception gap between project managers and their "missing customers"; providing an opportunity for PMs to excel again at over-delivering beyond the expectations of a static methodology and process.

Furthermore project managers should rise to the challenge of pushing the methodology they are governed by to the next evolution. Continuously strive to adjust, tweak, improve, to make better, enhance the way in which they execute to address and meet the real end user-user needs this industry should be leading with.

Lastly, and probably most importantly, as practitioners within an organisation or as practitioners working independently we should all look to push ourselves to be better than we were on the previous project.

This will make us unique and a true value for the end user: The ones we all work for.

These simple steps should resolve the mystery of missing customers on projects.

"Agile" Project Management Certification

Stephen Holton

> *Well, its finally happened... the Project Management Institute has given in and is creating an "Agile PM" certification. What a mess.*

I think far too many people out there fail to understand the difference between project methodologies and development approaches; hence the reason why we are seeing an "Agile PM Certification" and people talking about "Agile Project Management" - when there isn't such a thing.

It's like saying that there is "Waterfall Project Management" or "Software Development Life Cycle Project Management". These are just ways to approach the development of your deliverables; they are not project management methodologies in their own right (although the methodology needs to be adjusted to the needs of the development approach).

Furthermore, by raising a single development approach to the level of project methodology, we have hamstrung the possibility that people can choose multiple development approaches - depending on what best suits the needs of the various elements of the project (or even sub-projects), teams and customer requirements within the overall project/program structure.

Often the same project management methodology (adapted to the deliverable development approach) can be applied throughout - but highly structured sub-projects may benefit from a waterfall approach, while others may benefit from a more dynamic process such as Agile, iterative development and rapid prototyping. Still others require a structured design, test and deployment approach such as SDLC.

To raise the development approach to the same level as a project methodology not only mixes apples and oranges, it also ends up breaking the project – because the real objectives of project management aren't being met.

Developers are concerned with developing their deliverables within the context of the requirements; Project Managers are concerned that the development team is completing that task within the constraints of time, cost and quality. While the two groups overlap, there are also many distinct boundaries and priorities between them as well.

Unfortunately, the protectors of the project management body of knowledge have finally been harassed enough to hop onto the all-singing-all-dancing "Agile solution" to everyone's problems; we saw this with SDLC, and rapid prototyping, and now it's going to happen with Agile.

Let's face it – the project managers can't get rid of the developers (nor should they) and their coding standards, source safes, module libraries, etc. Nor should the developers invest so much time in trying to get rid of the project manager and project management.

It's a complimentary relationship – and instead of investing time on working together and reinforcing each other's weaknesses in approach, they are once again trying to do it alone.

We are stronger together than apart.

The "Supplemental" temporary/term employee; the worst of both worlds

Stephen Holton

Many people seeking employment these days are tempted by the question: do I want to be an independent contractor or an employee?

While the choice has always existed, many organizations are back to promoting a third option: contractual/term-employee (supplemental) – which may sound good for a short engagement, but could be costing you more than you think.

Let's put our roles in context first.

Employees

Employees are, for all intents a purposes, true servants (and beneficiaries of) the company they work for.

In exchange for regular employment, there are laws and standard practices that allow for minimum and maximum working hours, overtime, benefits, paid holidays, etc.

Similarly, you have a number of protections that apply against abuse, misuse, harassment, etc.

Contractors

Independent Contractors enjoy a different kind of relationship with the hiring organization; while generally appearing to be like an employee (working 9-5 beside their employee counterparts) they are still nominally engaged in a business-to-business relationship between the hiring organization and their own service delivery company (often consisting of just one employee – the contractor themselves) – although many contractors work through some 3rd party organization that serves as a placement/sourcing agency and "consolidator" for the end-client organization.

Many of the governing agreements and regulations concerning the engagement of the contractor are contained in the agreement between the employing organization and the service delivery company;

there may be no governing laws outside of general contract law.

As a result, the contractor usually does not get any holiday or sick days (or any benefits for that matter). While they don't get overtime, and they must be able to prove they worked for every hour they bill, they also get to bill for every hour they work (think about that carefully, especially when thinking of their salaried employee counterparts – who may be expected to work a lot of overtime, but are held to a fixed compensation level).

Now the contractor's home service delivery company that sent them to the hiring organization may be responsible for the standard employee benefits, and for adhering to the normal employment laws – but in reality, most contractors are independent, and therefore they own/manage their own companies; its hard to bring yourself to court for not paying you enough, giving you overtime or not recognizing your reasonable expectations of benefits.

That said, contractors generally enjoy a more lucrative revenue (although not necessarily salary), but they often do so at a cost in terms of the degree of effort they must put in for their end client, and the long periods between engagements where there may be no revenue coming in.

There are some other unique benefits however – such as being to write off various business expenses off of the pre-tax income of the company or contractor.

Term/Contractual Employees

As the name implies, term/contractual employees (also sometimes called "supplemental" employees) are individuals that are hired by companies on a short-term, contract basis.

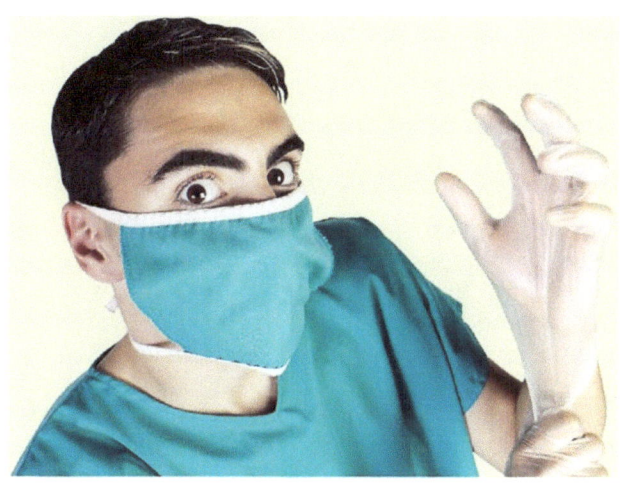

While they have the appearance of being employees in many cases, they are not fully employees, nor are they contractors.

These "supplemental" employees often work 9-5, and have their client take care of taxation issues such as deduction at source.

The client/employer however is rarely required (nor offers) any kind of health or medical coverage (just as if you were an independent consultant) or any vacation days (although, depending on the employment law in your region, the employer may be required to set aside a "vacation entitlement" of about 3-6% of your gross pay which you may be eligible to draw upon after a year of service – if you are still employed.

If not, then it is usually paid out upon the conclusion of your contract, or at the end of the fiscal year in which it was accrued.

The other problem that supplemental employees face is inequitable application of employee vs. contractor policies.

For instance – as a contractor, I must work every hour I invoice for, but I also get to invoice for every hour I work. As an employee, I'm given a fixed wage for 37.5 or 40 hours per week, and I'm generally expected to work at least those many hours. Some companies may even track hours, ensuring that you work every hour that you bill.

What has been a growing trend however is the concept of "inherent overtime" – where an employer expects the employee to put in extra hours above and beyond their 37.5/40 should it be necessary, and not expect any supplemental remuneration (ie- overtime, or time-off) as these periodic surges are inherent with their employment, but supposedly their additional efforts will be considered during

end-of-year employee reviews, and for the awarding of bonuses.

Supplemental employees often work on an hourly basis like contractors, but while they must work every hour they bill, they can't bill for every hour they work – because they are also expected to adhere to the inherent overtime rule.

This means that a supplemental who works only 35 hours in a given week can only bill for those 35 hours; but if they put in 45, they may be restricted to only billing 37.5/40.

The supplemental winds up being bound to the "inherent overtime" rule, but they are also term employees – so they don't get annual reviews, bonuses, etc. The only faint hope they have is that their additional efforts be recognized when considering them for continued employment.

One final threat to the supplemental or term employee is that in some jurisdictions (such as the Province of Quebec in Canada for instance), in order to minimize the risk of employers exploiting term/contract workers, they specifically prohibit continuous employment as a supplemental employee for any term longer than 2 years, lest the employer be forced to automatically convert the supplemental to employee status.

As a result, many employers will have a spontaneous renewal of supplemental employees every two years. Some have even gone so far as to extend this policy to their independent contractors – although it's not really required by law.

Comparison of "BENEFITS"

EMPLOYEE

Vacation:

Usually some, per your employment agreement as well as vacation-pay accrual under law.

Medical and other Benefits:

Yes, but the degree of benefits varies with each employer benefit package.

Expenses:

Usually reimbursement of pre-authorized, directly work-related expenses may be eligible.

Source Deductions (taxes taken automatically from your pay):

A requirement of the employer.

Other Issues:

May be subject to inherent overtime, but in consideration for annual reviews and bonuses.

CONSULTANT/INDEPENDENT CONTRACTOR

Vacation:

None.

Medical and other Benefits:

None, except what you arrange for yourself through your own company.

Expenses:

Some expenses may be billable back to your client, but all other expenses are at your discretion (and tax law) for expensing against your own company.

Source Deductions:

Your responsibility – and don't be late or miss them.

Other Issues:

Could be restricted to maximum of 2 year mandates with a single client.

Some governments also insist that you have multiple clients over a 3-5 year term, lest they assume you are just an "incorporated employee" – which is illegal.

TERM/SUPPLEMENTAL EMPLOYEE

Vacation:

Generally none, except maybe vacation-pay accrual under law

Medical and other Benefits:

Generally none, although some employers may allow you to "buy in" to their benefits program on a term basis, but this is rare.

Expenses:

Generally none, although some employers may allow work related expenses to be reimbursed per normal employee standards.

Source Deductions:

Yes, usually as a requirement of the employer.

Other Issues:

Often subject to inherent overtime expectations, but no annual review/bonus considerations – except possibly continued employment.

Some jurisdictions have specific limitations on maximum supplemental periods (ie- 2 years) with the same employer.

What Are The Advantages?

Employee vs. Contractor

This is the classic problem many people face; do I become a serf of the organization, or am I going to be a hired gun (or prostitute) hired out for a special job.

Tough call – and often it comes down to a combination of what benefits do you want/need vs. the rate and advantages of being independent (such as being able to write off almost anything associated with running your business).

Generally speaking, employees have the stability of a recurring paycheck and benefits.

Contractors, if the rate warrants, have their own corporation – and while they generally only have short-term engagements, they usually have much higher rates than employees and can afford time off between mandates to search for work.

They do, however, have the added burden of running their own company – including managing source deductions, government reports, book keeping and end of year accounting responsibilities.

Employee vs. Supplemental

Other than perhaps specifically enjoying a short term engagement (say working for the fall and winter and taking the spring and summer off) there really doesn't seem to be much advantage to the supplemental engagement – unless you really want to avoid the burden of running your own company – in which case you are nominally "outsourcing" the headache of bookkeeping, accounting and deductions at source to your employer.

Contractor vs. Supplemental

As with Employee vs. Supplemental – there appears to be no advantage, unless you are trying to avoid having to run you own company. Also keep in mind that you are losing out on the ability to write off your business expenses – such as travel, cell phone, some meals, paper, internet access (if you have a home office), etc.

Summary

Truthfully, short of being a retiree with few business expenses and no interest in running my own company, there is little or no advantage I can see to being a supplemental employee. I find such programs abusive of the good will and spirit of the employer/employee relationship.

Also be wary when negotiating such "supplemental"/term employee deals. The last one I had was established in good faith with a fortune 500 consulting firm – and they claimed to not know the specifics of the supplemental program, but sold it as being essentially just like being a contractor, and I could buy-into whatever employee programs I wanted if necessary. Worst case, I could even switch back to contractor if I chose.

Of course, it was nonsense... and contrary to what was implied, they had all the differences between the types of engagement at their fingertips.

Don't trust the recruiter – even when dealing with large, supposedly reputable firms. As always, get everything in writing, and weigh the advantages and disadvantages of the written agreement carefully before signing.

It's often what you aren't getting (such as write-offs, loss of overtime, forced maximum engagements, etc) that may be costing you more than you realize in the end.

Don Cherry for Order of Canada?

Stephen Holton

> *Why not? We used to recognize "leaders".*

Okay – I'll admit it. I'm as guilty as many others who simply dismiss Don Cherry as a loud mouth comic-book character who really isn't relevant to our daily lives outside of Canada's favorite sport (that's hockey for our American friends).

I may even, at times, have gone so far as to dismiss him (while doing my best "Grapes" impersonation) as "Kingston's favorite a—hole!"

Then a few weeks ago Mr. Cherry was nominated by the Royal Military College for an honorary Doctorate. Shortly after the announcement however – a teacher at the college challenged the nomination process (which was backed up by the 800 or so students attending the college, plus academics) – and a circus quickly ensued.

A few media outlets (most notably the Sun News Network) made a point of talking about Mr. Cherry's accomplishments, and questioning why no one was coming to his defence – after all the fanfare for his initial nomination.

In the end, Mr. Cherry politely declined the invitation – as he felt his presence would turn the event into a nightmare and take away from the other two recipients that had been selected for honorary degrees as well.

Well done and a class act by Mr. Cherry.

It was during this time that I started to learn some more about Don's background – and I wanted to share.

Born in Kingston Ontario on 5 February, 1934, Don has been a hockey player, coach and news commentator for nearly 60 years. Throughout all of this, first and foremost, he rarely minced words and never hesitated to tell you how he felt about something – regardless of whether it was politically correct or not.

What I didn't know however is that, outside of this TV-persona, Don is very active in a number of communities, charities, causes and associations. These activities include*:

- Lending his considerable persona to a number of selected charitable causes, most significantly, organ donation awareness.

- Establishing the Rose Cherry Home for Kids (in honor of his late wife).

- On November 14, 2005, Cherry was granted honorary membership of the Police Association of Ontario. Once an aspiring police officer, Cherry has been a long-time supporter of the police services.

- In June 2007, Cherry was made a Dominion Command Honorary Life Member of the Royal Canadian Legion in recognition of "his longstanding and unswerving support of ... Canadians in uniform".

- In February 2008, Cherry was awarded the Canadian Forces Medallion for Distinguished Service for 'unwavering support to men and women of the Canadian Forces, honouring fallen soldiers on his CBC broadcast during 'Coach's Corner' - a segment of Hockey Night in Canada'.

- In March 2010 the Canadian Broadcasting Corporation aired a 2 part documentary about Don called: "Keep Your Head Up, Kid: The Don Cherry Story"

Don also decided to spend Christmas 2010 with the troops in Afghanistan.

Don in Afghanistan   Source: thestar.com

Photo-Op or not (as some have suggested) he was in a WAR ZONE; something that not many of our so-called "leaders" are willing to do (with the notable exception of Peter MacKay, the Minister of National Defence, who has shown more intestinal fortitude than most of the others who have held the office put together).

The above list also doesn't even begin to address his considerable business, acting and other activities.

He's loud, politically incorrect, and obnoxious at times – but he's also a patriot, and generally tries to do good deeds (when not being a brash character on television).

I think that his greatest strength however is that whenever he has stepped over the line and gone a little too far, he's usually been pretty quick to stand up, make apologies, and then "soldier on" – doing what he loves, and still upsetting many in the process.

It takes a big man to say what he honestly thinks and feels; an even bigger one to admit when he's wrong.

More importantly however, whether you agree with him or not, I can't help but think his rough-edged honestly, patriotism and commitment to his community through charitable works distinguishes him for another award.

In October 2004, the CBC program The Greatest Canadian revealed that its 'top ten' viewer-selected great Canadians included Cherry. He finished seventh in the final tally, and is the only living member of the top 10 greatest Canadians who hasn't been awarded an Order of Canada.

From the Governor General's website, the Order is described as follows:

Established in 1967 by Her Majesty Queen Elizabeth II, the Order of Canada is the centrepiece of Canada's honours system and recognizes a lifetime of outstanding achievement, dedication to the community and service to the nation. The Order recognizes people in all sectors of Canadian society. Their contributions are varied, yet they have all enriched the lives of others and made a difference to this country. The Order of Canada's motto is DESIDERANTES MELIOREM PATRIAM (They desire a better country).

I don't see any particular requirement to be politically correct, well educated, always right, or perfect.

At one time we used to celebrate leaders who were brash, and tirelessly pushing forward against adversity.

Why, I've even heard it said that one of Canada's most popular Prime Ministers also created conflicting opinions throughout our country, and may have used the odd copulative adjective and singular finger gesture to express himself on occasion. He was awarded the Order.

I think the time is long overdue for the silent majority to push back against political correctness police and recognize a true leader; not perfect – but a decent and good man who does the best he can – and teaches as much from his good examples as he does when he recovers from his mistakes.

There's no doubt that Don has had to work hard for every benefit he's ever gotten – and in turn – has tried to return what he can to his community. In this "culture of entitlement" he's shown that you can still succeed through hard work and effort – and he has never let a setback keep him from what he loves to do.

Let us, as citizens, once again recognize a great Canadian and leader for the man he is; not some fictionalized, scrubbed, spin-controlled image that is neither realistic nor achievable.

Clearly I owe Mr. Cherry an apology.

Additionally I'd like to ask that anyone else who agrees that he's overdue - come join the cause at http://facebook.com/Don4OC.

Leaders are rare, and we should cherish them when we can; warts and all.

*with thanks to Wikipedia

Top 5 Consulting Scams

Stephen Holton

> *We've all heard the stories of the unscrupulous consultant who billed more hours than he actually put into a project; or the consultant who charges high rates for his work, and turns around and outsources the contract to a lower cost consultant or off-shore resource.*
>
> *The truth is there are a lot of other scams going on – and they aren't all being perpetuated by the consultants themselves.*

Now I want to start off by saying that there are a lot of ethical consultants and recruiters out there; the practices listed below aren't common across the industry – but they do occur. Knowing about them in advance is a great way to recognize and prepare yourself accordingly – whether as a vendor, or as a client.

All the examples are hypothetical of course; we're all friends here... so I'm borrowing liberally from academic examples. I've crossed my fingers as well.

www.despair.com

SCAM 1: The Kickback

Ever wonder where those huge markups some recruiters place on a contractors rate go? Especially if the only "service" provided by that recruiter is collecting a cheque from the client and

passing your share on to you – usually forcing you to wait the 30-days (+1 day for them to write a cheque) .

Well, in some cases, where multiple vendors are involved – each applies a markup to cover their "expenses" of maintain a sales force, office, etc. – and these multiple layers of markups have, on a few of my contracts, been as high as a 150% markup once everyone gets their cut (yes, that number is correct – I was being billed out at $2.50 for every 1.00 I billed).

Insane as it is, sometimes it takes multiple vendors leveraging their contacts to open the doors to a very lucrative client.

With single vendors however, it's harder to understand where that 30%plus markup goes (I'm talking 45-60 or more) – and in many cases it may just be going back to the hiring manager or procurement department with the client who, in turn, provides "preferential" treatment to some recruiters/vendors over others.

Look out for vendors that consistently win bids when they are often at a higher rate than others, or offer lower quality/less skilled consultants than other firms – but always seem to hold favor with key decision makers within the firm.

Likewise, if you know the rate being charged for the consultant is significantly higher than what you think the consultant is earning (not that you should be asking of course) – then be suspicious of the recruiter; unless they are offering lots of other incentives to the consultants, they could be exploiting them.

SCAM 2: Hiring manager is the recruiter

Sometimes discovering that the hiring manager knows every detail of your negotiations with the recruiter, in an embarrassing level of detail?

On at least one occasion, after some careful research, I discovered that the "president" of the preferred recruiting firm/vendor just happened to be the hiring manager (or family of the hiring manager).

Similar to "kickbacks" – in this scenario someone within the company is directly double-dipping; taking both a salary from the company, plus taking a cut of your contract fee as your recruiter/representative.

Research your recruiters thoroughly as part of the due diligence you should be doing with any new business contract. Getting to know your boss and some of the hiring staff isn't a bad idea either; they are going to Google you – doing the same back isn't necessarily a bad thing.

If you find a connection – get out. You could be implicated in the mess as well, and criminal charges are possible.

SCAM 3: Win and swap

This is similar to the recruiting scam of "bait and switch" – where an incredibly good "potential" offer is put on the table by a recruiter as an incentive to join them on a bid; once they get the contract however, they turn around and offer the position to a less senior (and less costly) resource.

From the hiring organization's perspective they award a "win" to a vendor – and the vendor advises that the consultant whose resume was attached to the bid is no longer available; but, in accordance with the contract, they will provide an "alternate". This alternate, however, is often at a lower rate to the vendor - but the contract rate to the client/employer is not adjusted accordingly.

Be wary of these alternates, and ensure that your initial request for proposal includes the fact that you get to assess the suitability of any replacement contractors/resources due to lack of availability post-contract award. Always have the ability to terminate the contract, adjust rates or change vendors should you find that the proposed very senior resource is no longer available.

SCAM 4: Leveraging what you don't know

Hey... we often hire consultants to bring us experience and skills that we don't already have in the organization, and may not be able to afford in a long-term permanent resource; it goes to the heart of why we use consultants.

But be wary of those consultants who exploit the gats in knowledge of your employees.

I knew of one consultant who, during a financial crisis with his client, would go to great lengths to ensure they saw him finding ways to cut a few thousand here and there in savings from their primary outsourcer (a large international business machines company that I won't name).

What the client didn't realize (a former government organization, whose employees didn't always understand the subtleties of cost of ownership and return on investment) that much of this consultants work was actually "billable effort" to the outsourcer

(by using time and effort of front line delivery and support teams).

As a result, the client was actually SPENDING more money than they were getting back in savings.

Now, that's not to say that there weren't ways to secure those savings – by engaging business/portfolio managers and other customer relationship management teams between the client and the outsourcing partner.

The problem with that approach, of course, is that the consultant wouldn't be able to readily claim that HE personally saved the client thousands of dollars at the end of the day.

He put his own interests before those of his client – and at their cost.

More interesting of course is the fact that one of the previous clients of that consultant happened to be that outsourcing company – so it's not as if he didn't know what he was doing was wrong in the first place.

SCAM 5: *Learning on your dime*

Sometimes you can't get employees or consultants who are already highly skilled with your new system, service or tools – so you need to train them or, at the minimum, give them time to gain experience and confidence with those new tools.

While there's nothing wrong with that scenario – just be careful to ensure that you aren't necessarily taking on the full burden for training a vendor's team and giving them skills that they can turn around and sell elsewhere on your dime.

If it's a long term engagement you have with the vendor, or it's a unique system/service not readily used elsewhere (or again) – then fine; you should carry the burden. If, however, this is a short engagement, and the training creates significant value for the vendor, it would not be unreasonable to expect some kind of discount or reduced pricing on the time of the staff while they are being trained (and before they can bring their full value to bear for you).

During the height of the PeopleSoft/SAP/other ERP craze, many many integrators exploited their clients for training and experience – often slipping a junior into the team – but billing them at top rate as they gained the hands-on experience they needed to really be useful post training.

A BONUS SCAM

I couldn't resist throwing in a "bonus" one – and I'm not quite sure how to fit this one in – but it's great, and subtle.

Senior Manager X decides to launch a multi-year project just prior to his retirement.

He selects an independent contractor to take on the assignment at a very good rate.

Now after a year the senior manager retires, The organization has a standing order that retirees cannot immediately return as contractors without either at least a 1 year break of employment, or special (and difficult to get) waivers from the most senior levels.

Oddly enough, however, due to the background knowledge and history retained by this former manager, he turns out to be the "ideal" candidate to become the assistant to the contractor – and since this was technically a different company in an existing B2B relationship, not technically a conflict under the rules.

CONCLUSION

Now don't get too depressed; I've generally found more ethical individuals than unethical ones in my 20+ years as a consultant/professional.

That said, situations like these do happen – but they are the exception. Knowing what to look for in advance can help you prepare, and take action if necessary.

Tips and Tricks

The "(l)earned value" (a play on project management terminology) section of our website featured a number of tips, tricks and lessons learned for a variety of business and project management problems.

We've only posted a few this year – with more planned to come out with the introduction of our new/standardized project methodology (small-pm) in 2012.

Quick capture solution for white boarders...

Stephen Holton

What did we do before whiteboards? It's hard to imagine some days. Despite us supposedly entering an era of technology and the (eventual) paperless office – it seems that we always wind up going back to our most fundamental roots and start making the cave-drawings on the walls again. The problem, of course, is after the meeting – and whatever poor schmuck is stuck with capturing the minutes after the fact.

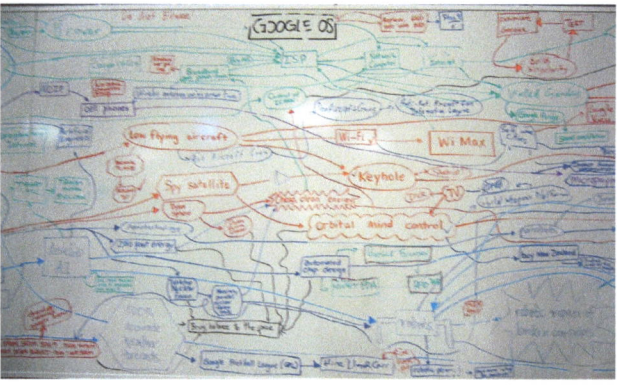

Many of us try to capture the drawings as they are developed; or stay afterwards to draw what was left on the board (and hopefully make sense of it as well).

Embarrassingly enough a tech writer pointed out an ingenious (and admittedly obvious) solution; just use my digital camera.

At the time, digital cameras were still stand-alone items... but today with these cameras being incorporated into a variety of devices (including that cell phone that is probably permanently attached to your ear) – there is little excuse for not rapidly capturing your meeting cave-drawings.

Keep in mind the following however:

- the flash may obscure some parts of your diagram; so take multiple shots (this is also good if you have a shaky hand)

- you may need to take different shots – up close and some all-encompassing – in order to get a clear picture of the work

- don't forget to erase the board when done – but only after checking to ensure your pictures are clear and usable

The extra advantage to this approach is that you only need attach the pictures to your meeting minutes/records of decisions you send out after – and may just get away without having to spend hours recreating diagrams in whatever presentation software your office uses.

Happy white boarding.

"Minuiting" Documents

Stephen Holton

I never cease to be amazed at how much paper is on my desk and inundating my project files despite living in this "paperless" era.

Post-Its aside (which invariably disappear when you need them most) one of the key problems that many of us encounter is how to keep track of updates and other various notations on activities/events with a paper document.

Now admittedly there are organizations that employ complex document management systems that do, indeed, scan in such noxious pieces of paper for storage, retention, forwarding and annotation – but unless you are lucky/unlucky enough to be burdened with such a system, and haven't elected to burn out your own scanner and fill up your local disk drives – the question remains: how do you annotate documents and "circulate" them for action within your team/organization?

The military dealt with this problem through a process called "minuting" – where numbered notations were made on the face of a document that addressed to-dos to individuals within the team/organization, and their responses until – ultimately – the document was "retired" to central records for retention/storage.

How It's Done

Every original document starts off as the original minute #1.

Subsequent minutes are numbered successfully (2, 3, 4 etc) and follow the same general format:

> <#> <Addressee>
> <minute text – instruction, note, action, etc>
> <signature/date>

Often people will cross out the number on the previous minute – so you can readily find the next one that is "current" on the page.

They can also be placed pretty much anywhere on the page – wherever there is an open space to make your next item.

Adding a "Note to File" (NTF)

A special "addressee" of a minute is the file/document itself – the NOTE TO FILE – where you can append notes and general information/history into your minuiting records.

Strengths

Minutes provide a quick means to send out action items and have a traceable history for non-electronic documents – without the mess (and potential loss) of Post-Its or other attachments.

Shortcomings

It's critical that everyone "respects" an original document – recognizing that it may be the only existing history of actions and events associated with the original subject.

As a result, not only should people keep track of whatever "minuted" documents they have in circulation – they have to be cognizant that it may be necessary to retain the original document after it's been circulated and acted upon to retain the record of what happened.

Now in some cases this is the time that you may want to scan the final draft – and then retain an electronic image of the final document within your electronic document repository.

While this is a good strategy for long term record keeping – you then need to also consider either the destruction or, at least isolation of that original document (lest someone add additional minutes) resulting in a variance between the electric archived copy and the original (which may start an all new round of circulation).

Conclusion

Ultimately this was a technique best used within small teams – and remains so today. Consider its inclusion as a tool/technique within your project management communication strategy – but pay attention to that long term retention plan.

Meeting Invitations

Michael Netto

So there you are, scanning through the myriad of endless emails in your inbox, as you do each and every morning.

As fate would have it, there they are waiting amongst the email onslaught. Much like young children waiting behind fortified snow hills, snowballs prepared in advance for the unsuspecting character to wander by: the often dreaded meeting invitation.

Since you obviously don't have enough meetings to already attend, you are quick to click on the Accept button. But what exactly did you just accept? And why?

As is quickly becoming the norm, you don't really know, do you?

We have all received those invitations. Yes, the time and date are there. You may even see a few other attendees listed. The subject line is usually filled in, but may be as generic as "Discuss the Project" (of which project you will certainly know, since you are only involved in five this week). Finally, since there is no room booked or call-in information available, you know that we will all be expected to work on fine-tuning our telepathy capabilities before the meeting.

Perhaps it is a result of the absolute frantic pace in which we all work today, that many of us send meeting invitations to one another without much thought to an explanation of why we need to come together in a closed room to exchange information and ideas - or to make a decision about something vitally important to the organization.

Whatever the cause, it is quite apparent that the behaviour needs to change, if not for efficiency in the workplace, well then maybe for something as forgotten and rare as politeness.

I'd like to share with you a few simple ideas for those times that you will be manipulating Microsoft Outlook or Lotus Notes to get one of these invites out to a group of your nearest and dearest. You want to be as informative as possible, giving the requested attendees the very best reason why they should choose to attend your meeting over the other ones they receive.

Yes, believe it or not, they often are double and triple-booked, and will cognitively choose where they need to be.

Here is what should be among the elements in every meeting invite that you prepare from now on.

- The Non-cryptic Subject Line
- The Meeting Objective
- The Expected Meeting Outcome
- The Attendee List (optional / required)
- The Frequency and Location
- Call-In Information
- Supporting Documentation / Web Sites

Although this may appear heavy at first glance, you will quickly realize (during your application of this in your daily life) that the "copy and paste" function available on most computers is actually not that difficult to master. Let's go through each of these elements in detail.

The Non-Cryptic Subject Line

As was touched on a bit earlier, you want to make sure that your audience understands how this email invitation fits into their workload. Distance yourself from the generic titles such as "Meeting about Project Issue."

Remember, your invite will be buried amidst hundreds of other emails, and your audience wants to be able to quickly decipher what they are about to read. Context is everything, isn't it?

Couple that with the proliferation of handheld devices and you definitely have trouble. Imagine, if you will, a busy executive leaving a meeting, grabbing her blackberry to check for what/where/when details on the next meeting. Hhhmm, let's see, a meeting on "Meeting about Project Issue." Yup, that's not cryptic at all.

Instead, offer your participants some information, but keep it concise. I usually maintain the following nomenclature on Subject Lines: "Project Name – Meeting Name – Topic, if necessary," which results in something like "Project Genesis – Biweekly Core Team Status Meeting."

The Meeting Objective

Your audience deserves an explanation as to why this meeting needs to happen. Equally, why you deserve their attendance and participation. Meetings come in a few flavours:

- **Informative:** One-way sharing of information, where the speaker "enlightens" the audience on a subject of interest

- **Brainstorming:** A meeting of the minds and spirits, to gather as many ideas as possible. This is also referred to as white-boarding, where we all grab dry-erase markers and take our turns at understanding one another's icons (and hieroglyphics)

- **Analysis:** Taking any idea and breaking it down into choices and elements, weighing the pros and cons of each. This usually results in the scheduling of subsequent "analysis" meetings. It's infinitely recursive, we all realize, yet we enjoy the practice, let alone the time in a closed conference room to enjoy fresh-brewed java.

- **Status:** Ah, the Project Manager's favourite meeting. Ah, the delivery team's least-favourite meeting. This is the ultimate "what are you working on and why are you late again?" back and forth meeting that we've all become accustomed to. We take turns surfing on our laptops when it's not our turn to provide status on the deliverable of the moment.

- **Decision Making:** Perhaps the most under-used, the Decision Making meeting is often the most politically challenging one available for us to schedule. Gulp, someone's going to make an actual decision?! Egads! Will that mean there's accountability after the meeting, and that the giant wheel will turn a few clicks?

- **The Mixed Bag:** Sometimes, just sometimes, we need to realize that we are, indeed, capable of accomplishing a few things within the confines of one specific meeting.

Make sure that you tell the participants what type of meeting you need to have. Meetings have been derailed for far less a reason. It's always nice to remind rambling folk that "we are gathered here to make a decision on this, and not to debate its merit." We all know those individuals who love to hear themselves talk. I firmly believe that every organization should have some sort of quota to meet in regards to that archetype.

The Expected Meeting Outcome

Be specific here. This element underlines the value of this meeting to the business. You may even want to further state what may be the result of a failure to

meet the outcome. Whatever the reason for the meeting, it needs to get done. Unless, of course, it doesn't need to get done – at which point you should question why you are scheduling a meeting in the very first place. Uh-hum...

The Attendee List

I'm sure you've all heard it. The "Do I really have to attend your meeting?" line that comes at us from all angles. If I had a nickel for every time that someone said "I can't wait to attend your meeting", well, then, I wouldn't have any nickels.

I usually use the mail client's TO: and CC: features to cover this, but I explain my lapse in depth of logic within the email itself, using this element to cover it off. Those CCd are optional. Those TOd are not.

I often also insert a "Do Not Forward" statement on some instances of invitations. I've often been amazed at how unknown individuals start to show up at certain meetings I've chaired, with the meeting becoming a standing-room only event. I didn't realize that I was such a sought-after speaker. Maybe I should start charging?

As a last note, we've all received wedding invitations (if you haven't, lucky you!). We all know that we are supposed to RSVP. For some insane reason, I expect people at work to use that same logic. RSVP. Such a foreign concept, indeed!

Okay, so that wasn't a last note. This one is though: For those of you that enjoy the "Decline" option of an invitation, in the spirit of over-communicating, you may want to explain to the meeting chair why you are declining. I love receiving a decline note with no explanation. It gives me the warm and fuzzies.

The Frequency and Location

Very simply put, it's nice to set the expectation from the get go. Will this be a monthly meeting? Biweekly? Ad-Hoc? It simply puts people into context. It also avoids the "Oh, I didn't realize that this was a recurring meeting!" Consider integrating the "frequency" into your Subject Line, such as "Biweekly Status Meeting."

Yes, it's also incumbent on you to use the "recurring" feature of your email client. Lock the participants in! However, you may have a more difficult time with the conference rooms. Many organizations now allow scheduling of rooms as "resources" within email.

It's not always easy or feasible to reserve a specific room every Wednesday morning at 7am, given how much people love 7am meetings. Yes, elbow grease may be required at this point. You have options. Send separate email invitations for each recurrence, using different rooms. Barter with your peers to get the room you need. Meet at the bar across the street. Or better yet, barter at the bar across the street.

If you will be scheduling a remote team, and you are able to reserve a conference room in that location as well, it might be a good idea to reserve a room on their behalf. By having remote participants in a common room, they are more likely to be actively engaged in the conversation (rather than scanning through email at their desk while on the conference bridge, muttering their hmm-hmmm's ever so often to keep you thinking they care).

Oh, people who sit a few feet over from you or on another floor in the same building don't qualify as "remote participants." They need to attend in person. They should not be permitted to call into the conference bridge from their desk, as that leads to the same disengagement and lower quality communications that sometimes results with remote teams. Plus, the extra few feet of walking to that conference room can move them over the top of that much-hyped guideline of 10,000 steps daily!

Call-In Information

You have invited people from different time zones to your meeting, as is becoming the case with this virtual wired world in which we reside. The meeting starts. You wait for everyone to join. Suddenly, urgent emails flow in, your cellular starts to vibrate with incoming calls and text messages. That 1-800 number that works in your location ONLY works in your location.

Don't assume that it will work in Canada if you are in the US. Apparently, it may also not work in the US if you live in Canada. Do I really need to speak of the intricacies involved with the telecommunications networks in the rest of the world? While we're at it, you may want to provide "local" call-in numbers, since carriers sometimes won't allow a 1-800 number within a local calling area.

Supporting Documentation / Web Sites

Instead of sending your supporting documents within the invitation or by email, make them available for download on your corporate intranet, portal, or shared virtual space in whatever cloud that exists for you. Make reference to this within your invite. Finally, if you want your meeting to be productive and without the noise of frantic paper-rustling, endeavour to make the reference material available a full 24 hours in advance of the meeting.

In Conclusion

I know what you're thinking - I'm crazy. There is no way this can be efficient. Way to heavy to use in a practical context! Go ahead, keep not doing what you are not doing, and reap the results of that. If you change your mind and you are interested in introducing some efficiency and politeness in the way we all work together as human beings, give this a try. Let me know what different things that you've tried work for you. I'd love to exchange, learn and adapt my own way of working.

And to save you some time, I'll leave you with the following. A simple "copy and paste" into the body of your invitation will have you up and running in mere seconds, leaving you time to attend more of your favourite meetings!

Feel free to contact me at mnetto@mentisor.com . Or better yet, schedule a meeting today!

Sample Body of an Effective Email Invitation Template

Try a quick copy/paste into your next invitation, and see how easy this really is.

The Meeting Objective:

This is a Status Meeting. Each team member will provide informative insight with respect to their current activities, with special focus and notes on any issues or risks. Please come prepared with sufficient details to share (such as dates). There will also be a decision point towards the end of the meeting with regards to selecting Option A or B.

Expected Meeting Outcome

Formal Decision on Option A or Option B, followed by execution of that option after the meeting. If a Decision is not reached, we will not meet our target date promised to the Executive Committee.

The Attendee List (optional / required)

All member of the core team are expected to attend. Please delegate to someone, if you cannot attend.

Those invitees cc'd on this invitation are optional.

Please do not forward this invitation to anyone other than a named delegate.

Frequency and Location

This meeting is held every Monday at 3pm. On Holiday Mondays, this meeting will be rescheduled to the following Tuesday.

Call-In Information

North American Toll Free: 1-800-555-1212

England Toll Free: 011-44-124-13233

Local City: 514-555-1212

Participant Passcode: 987 6543

Supporting Documentation / Web Sites

Please see current word doc on project folder on shared drive, subfolder titled `"Meetings" with today's date

The Result

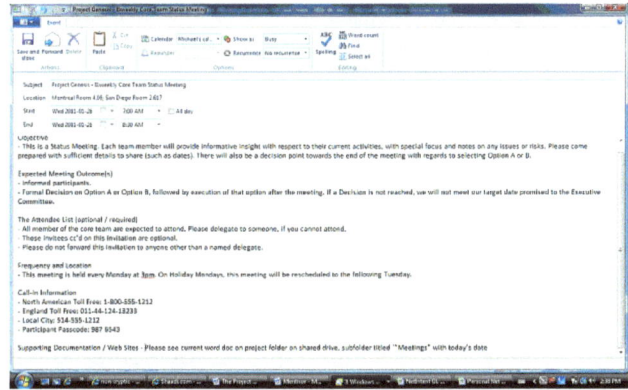

Quick Meeting Minutes

Stephen Holton

I'll admit it; I was notoriously bad for not writing up minutes or records of decision after meetings (I'll leave the distraction between the two for a future article).

I've gotten much better in recent years – due in part to using the actual original meeting invitation (assuming you issued one electronically) as part of the solution/quick fix.

Most electronic calendars/email packages (including Outlook, Lotus Notes, etc) have an option

where you can send an email to all invitees of a meeting.

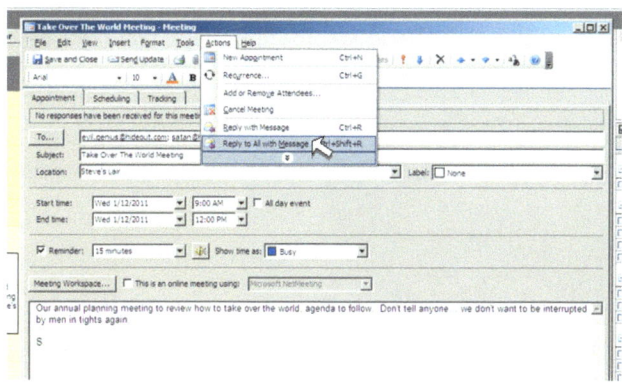

The technique is relatively simple; reply to everyone on the original meeting list – and use the list of addresses to help form your "attendee" checklist in the body of your message.

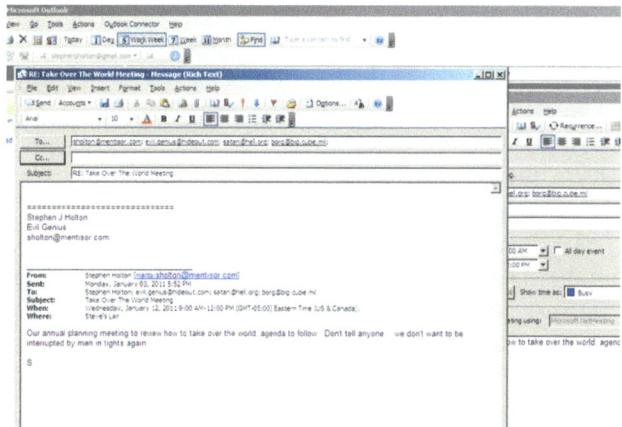

As attendees join the meeting – you can simply "check" them off – by adding a Y or N (or blank) beside their name to register their attendance.

Add a simple text template to keep track of the agenda, record of decisions, summary of next steps and then (perhaps the hardest part) – actually USE your computer during the meeting to keep notes as you proceed (this can be tricky for those who may be two-finger typists, but you can get an assistant or PCO to do this as well).

Important Tips

- Remember to use the template as a tool to organize your thoughts prior to and during the meeting.\

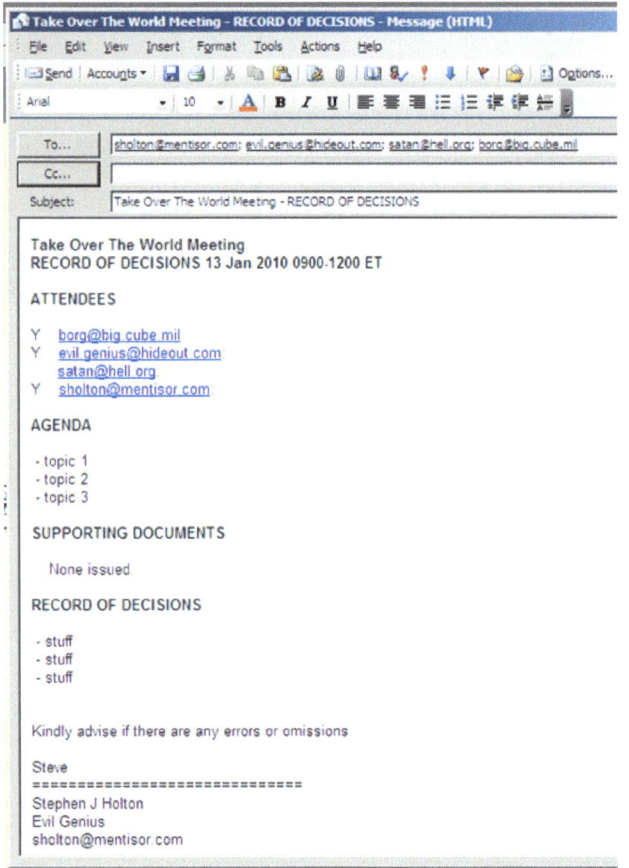

MEETING XYZ (usually taken from the subject line of the original message)

RECORD OF DECISIONS <put in the date/time of the meeting>

ATTENDEES

(this is where the block of email addresses comes in handy; now just indent them one tab and put a Y or N in as they attend your meeting)

AGENDA

(bulleted list of agenda items – if you have one)

SUPPORTING DOCUMENTS

(you may want to re-attach reference documents issued before or during the meeting; remember to indicate if they have been updated since the initial release – possibly from discussions during the meeting)

RECORD OF DECISIONS/DISCUSSIONS

(I usually start off by cutting and pasting my agenda here; then that becomes level 0 of my bulleted list/outline of discussions – which I'm noting throughout the meeting. Its also okay to stop the meeting and ask for everyone's thoughts/input on the best way to summarize the outcome of a discussion)

SUMMARY OF MAJOR ACTION ITEMS

(this isn't always necessary – but it's a nice touch if you really want to emphasize who is doing what; especially if you don't have an issues & actions log to release)

NEXT SCHEDULED MEETING

(manage expectations; even if the next meeting isn't set or known – at least state who will organize the next one if/when it is required)

- Don't waste a lot of time on making perfect notes on the initial pass; just use point form and get into the habit of using indents to handle sub-topics/side-discussions related to a particular topic (much like the "outlining" method for creating a document).

- Remember that you will have a chance after the meeting to refine your notes a little further before pressing send.

The advantage of this approach, if you are disciplined and have the necessary keyboarding skills, is that you can get meeting minutes/records of decision out quickly (within a few minutes to a few hours) of a meeting being held.

Basic Template

I've gotten to the point that I can pretty much do the template on the fly – as I pretty much have it memorized. Until you reach that point however, you can cut and paste from here to help you:

Finally, I like to add the following at the end:

Kindly advise if I've made any errors or

omissions; reply to all if the matter is particularly important/urgent.

Conclusion

Don't forget to review the distribution list just before you send out your notes; often there are people who were not invited to the meeting (and therefore won't be on your distribution list) that may need to be added – just as a courtesy or for information purposes.

While this technique doesn't make writing meeting minutes/records of decision any better, it tends to suck a little less – and you look like a hero to your team when you can get them out in a matter of minutes or hours vs. the days (or never) like many others.

Best (and no so Best) of the Mentisor Soapbox

The Soapbox is our weekly internet-based "radio" show/podcast that can be found on-line at http://www.blogtalkradio.com/Mentisor.

Here the Mentisor team takes on a variety of subjects – and usually have a good opportunity to take a few jabs at each other in the process.

Additionally, having the perfect bodies for radio work, the team maintains that they do the entire show naked in order to increase market-share.

Some of the Best

Some of our best topics so far have been the recurring segments where we explore a broad set of topics usually within a single discipline; this includes:

- Analysis of the Principles of Leadership
- Analysis of the 5 Dysfunctions of a Team (based upon the work of Patrick Lencioni)
- Harold Kerzner's 20 Mistakes of New/Novice Project Managers

Not all of these have been stellar however – with perhaps our biggest flop being an analysis of Richard Greene's 48 Laws of Power which, after the first 12, we quickly realized was a relatively pedantic and conflicting list.

Other great topics over the first year and a half have included:

- Discussion about the dismissal of Captain Honors of the USS Enterprise
- Tools/techniques for Stakeholder Analysis
- Soft skills necessary for management success

Advertising Challenges

Being an on-line show, advertising on-line through social media tends to make sense – and has proven to be quite successful for both our Facebook page, as well as increasing listenership on our show (we are starting to suspect that the "naked" part isn't really cutting it).

That said, who would have believed that Facebook actually have "nipple police" – and it took some effort to get our original ad approved by the morality squad:

The "banned" Facebook ad... no nipples please.

It seems that it's oaky to show a girl in a skimpy bikini and promise to give you bigger body parts, or to teach you the top 3 words to get any woman into bed, but essentially a picture of a man wearing his beachwear doesn't count it.

Crop the shot just a little – and suddenly its all moral and acceptable. Go figure.

Oh… and we think the 3 words are: "I'm a consultant".

Other Oddities

No mention of "oddities" would be complete without mentioning Doctor Project.

Originally intended as a semi-serious segment where we would attempt to answer real questions from the audience about project management – we've pretty much been off the rails from the onset, and have been having fun ever since.

Doctor Project has his own Facebook and YouTube pages, but admittedly we just haven't had much time to maintain them.

Perhaps as his popularity grows, you too can seek out his interesting solutions and advice to the most troubling problems that affect business and society in general today.

Dr. Project
…and the other Mentisor Soapbox guys.

Lunchtime-Mondays 12-1pm ET
www.blogtalkradio.com/mentisor

www.Mentisor.com

Help! We've been Blogged!!

Okay – so I'll admit our experiment with blogging didn't go well. It's not that we aren't willing to write, or provide content – but the engine we were using was just not easy to use as a "group" publishing tool.

BLOGGING

WE'RE GOING TO NEED MORE MONKEYS.

That said, there were some good entries – most notably the Wiki hacking primer that we've converted to two full articles in the earlier section.

Here are some of the other missives and rants that followed.

(you may want to note that we've switched to using our Facebook page for these posts/updates– as it tends to be more "viral").

So a recruiter calls me today...

Michael Netto

I am seriously beginning to dread recruiter calls. Yes, they may eventually help me to find a new client, but wow is it painful...

Today, the phone rings, and there's that friendly voice of another recruiter who has found my profile on LinkedIn or monster, and is sure I am a perfect

fit for a new role they are working to fill. Would I like to hear it? Well, of course I would.

"Seeking a PCO or PMO to manage mutli-stream and multi-project environment. Must have worked with staff of 75. Experience in the Financial Services Sector required. One year contract."

Ummm, okay, PCO or PMO? What? Do you mean "or PM"? No? Oh...

Worked with staff of 75? What do you mean "with"? Oh, you don't know? Oh...

And it's a big 5 Consulting Company, with a lower-Manhattan investment bank as a client? Nice! Sounds impressive. Oh, they pay that little per hour on contract? Oh... Better not be in USD...

Guess I shouldn't ask for an elaboration on the multi-stream, multi-project thing.

A perfect fit, huh?

PMs should NOT do minutes

Bob Dunstall

Which isn't what every project team you've ever worked with will tell you. Of course the PM does the minutes!   But in reality what the PM should do is to set the agenda and then drive the meeting to achieve results.

That doesn't give you time to take effective notes and produce decent minutes.

It should in fact be assigned by the PM, work allocation, to one of the other team members perhaps on a rotating basis. (and of course the PM then does need to follow up to make sure it gets done.)

It's also part of the need for the PM to husband the precious time you have available to direct the project.

One thing most PMs are critically aware of is that the percentage of the total project budget that is allocated to project management is continuously and rigorously scrutinized by our clients.

So you need to ensure that not only are you getting a bang for your buck from your project resources but also that you are getting the biggest bang possible for yourself.

Your tax dollars at work...

My wife attempted to register a business with the government yesterday – only to discover that they have switched to a "paperless" registration system as of January, and that it hasn't been working.

The computers are down, and they've already disposed of all the old paper forms that were part of the manual process used previously.

The employees we spoke with indicated this has been going on for a month.

First, who disposes of a manual process before a new automated one has been fully tested and validated? That goes against over 30 years of software development practices.

Secondly, what are all the employees doing – who appear to be stuck unable to help anyone? It's not their fault of course, but that's a lot of salaries being paid out for people to sit, answer phones, and explain they can't do anything.

Third, what software firm won this contract, and what is being done to penalize them for this misconduct (especially penalties for the salaries of government employees who are waiting for the system to be fixed).

In these economic times, considering that small businesses create the majority of jobs in most economies, it's amazing that the government first of all got itself into this mess, and equally amazing that someone hasn't just hasn't printed/photocopied more of the original forms and maintained the manual process for a little while longer.

I trust the government will be taking some appropriate action soon, including perhaps rethinking some senior appointments that have been involved with this fiasco.

I suspect nothing will be done of course; this isn't the first government IT project to go belly-up.

Saved by the backup...

Stephen Holton

Every now and then, I really pooch-it when it comes to managing systems or sites, and once again I'm pleased to acknowledge that a good backup scheme saved by backside yet again.

I wanted to upgrade the Mentisor site to the latest version of Joomla – but I got lazy and thought I would trust the automated scripts that my hosting provider has on their site. I knew it was probably a bad idea, and despite some initial hiccups, I thought it had done the upgrade successfully.

Well, of course, it hadn't. There were little disconnects that were only discovered a few days later.

Fortunately I had the presence of mind to make a backup just before doing the site upgrade.

Never underestimate the value of a complete backup – especially before what should be a minor upgrade.

In any case, for anyone who manages a Joomla based site – I can't say enough good things about "Akeeba Backup" – a free component that does a complete site (including database) backup and restore.

I've used it not just for site restorations – but also complete site moves.

It's a great tool – and supported as "donation-ware". So give it a try, and if you like it, remember to support the developer.

He saved my backside – and I'll be making my donation this week.

Mentisor Contributors

Bob Dunstall, PMP

Bob Dunstall is one of the most experienced members of the Mentisor team – having both his Project Management Professional designation, as well as certified as an IBM Executive Project Manager.

He has a solid and proven track record of delivering the large complex projects for both software development and services organizations.

As a program manager for IBM, he directed the implementation of a major transition project that resulted in annual client savings of $40 million with a project budget in excess of $10 million and met a very challenging delivery schedule.

For Essentus he met critical delivery schedules for two major retail software development projects with over 100 developers in multiple teams in Canada, Europe and India.

As key business integration executive for operational systems at CP Rail, achieved improvements in asset utilization and efficiencies in terminal facilities through technology spin-offs from our implementation of the industries Positive Train Control prototype ATCS.

A proven team-builder, Bob enjoys managing and leading in diverse cultural environments and the challenges and rewards of motivating exceptional people.

Stephen Holton, PMP, CISSP, SSGB, ITIL, CD

After completing over twelve years' service in the Canadian Armed Forces, Stephen moved to private industry where he was employed as a Director of Information Technology, Director of Operations and CIO for a number of private sector companies before finally electing to become an independent consultant in 2000.

Since then he's served as a management consultant, project/program manager and business analyst/solution architect in a number of industries and organizations - including a big-5 consulting firm.

These industries and organizations have included the airline, railway, telecommunications and banking industries, the Canadian and US Governments, as well as mandates in Brazil and Bermuda.

Frederic Lempereur, PMP

Frederic has been a project manager since 1997, and was certified as a PMP in 2003.

He has primarily focussed in infrastructure service projects, but has adapted his tools, techniques and processes to facilitate organizational change and to support events.

He has been actively involved in the design and improvement of PMO processes, organization, and has served as a portfolio lead managing teams of project managers and integrating their projects/activities against a broad array of customer requirements and profiles.

Fred loves a healthy debate on good project management and its values. He's less accepting of Project Managers who feel superior based on certifications or diplomas without solid street knowledge to back it up, but finds those willing to want to learn and change a refreshing and welcome addition to his team.

Michael Netto, PMP

Michael has almost 20 years of experience across a variety of industries, including IT, management consulting, air transport, banking, loyalty management, and media broadcasting. He has been deeply involved and passionate in the field of Project Management since 1998 and earned his PMP designation in early 2002. Michael is a graduate of McGill University's Business School, having earned a Bachelor of Commerce Degree in Information Systems. He had also certified as a Novell Engineer in the mid-1990s.

Michael has held roles with multinationals such as IBM, Compuware and Siemens AG, and he has worked in leadership positions in their respective IT Delivery Organizations.

Currently, Michael lives and works in Montreal, Quebec, Canada as an independent Project Management Consultant. He is also co-host of a weekly internet radio forum for Senior IT and business professionals, which takes a light hearted stab at discussions affecting the business, IT and consulting industries

Fred Parker

Fred has been Moderating on, and Administrating Private and Public Forums and BBS for well over a decade, and in recent years has been dabbling in creating websites with Wiki and/or social-networking tools, mostly creating and guiding the evolution of "hobby" Communities.

Currently he is spearheading an ambitious world-wide Community and Wiki website based on, and loosely partnered with an emerging virtual-gaming leader, with a ground-breaking first-person, yet team-based Online-Game that will soon be out of Beta-phase!

Security has always been an interest and hobby for Fred, but with his new on-line community activities – it has become a necessity.

Patrick Richard, PEng, PMP

A Project Manager and Technical Lead in a wide variety of applications centered on pharma, biotech, food, and beverage manufacturing.

He is particularly interested in ERP to plant floor integration, manufacturing data valorization, and Key Performance Indicators.

He is also focused on serving Canadian industry and the project management profession, and in addition to his Mentisor contributions – maintains his own very active LinkedIn group (CanadianPM) and a regular blog (Hardnosed PM).

Patrick's specialties include Manufacturing IT for the Pharmaceuticals, Food and Beverages, Cement, and Pulp and Paper industries.

Special Guests & Supporters

We've had a number of special guests on the Soapbox as well, including:

- Peter Bauer
- David Beaumier
- Martin Buckland, Executive Career Management Services Professional
- Paul Fritz-Nemeth
- Brian Meredith
- John Miller
- George Polsky
- Brad Szollose, Award winning author of Liquid Leadership: From Woodstock to Wikipedia
- Roslyn Takeishi
- Jeffrey Taylor, Lobbyist and Managing Partner; U.S. Government Relations Intl., LLC
- George Worrell, Media/Event planner and Style Consultant

Most importantly, we want to thank the staff of the Montreal Hotel-Y who have tolerated our antics, have been quick to support us during "emergencies", and have generally been great about helping host our weekly Soapbox radio shows.

The Final Word

It's proven to be an exciting start for Mentisor, and now the question is where does this little start up go from here?

First and foremost, with the initial successes we've enjoyed with BlogTalkRadio, we want to expand our shows – and in 2012 will be hosting:

- **The Soapbox –** with our usual gang of consultants and thugs, duking it out over various business, technology and leadership issues of the day.

- **Private Spaces –** discussing privacy and security in your personal and private lives – and showing that education and knowledge is the best way to ensure (and insure) protection against the usual hype leading to just more fear, uncertainly and doubt (FUD).

- **Inside Style –** with George Worrell, a Nationally known style and fashion consultant in Washington DC, we discuss various culture, lifestyle and etiquette issues and just plan living well.

We're also starting to move away from just being source of knowledge, but also expanding our services to include new website and capabilities, such as:

- **ExecutiveOutcomes.com –** our new portal for turn-key solutions and management consulting services, including:
    - Access to senior consultants and professionals to resolve your major business, technology or management problems
    - On-Line survey services to canvass customers, internal teams or the market at general.
    - Social-Media integration services – both education and hands-on delivery.
    - On-line education services - both instructor-led, as well as computer based training and evaluations; a great tool for helping minimize the ongoing costs of annual refreshers on key policies such as harassment awareness, or onboarding of employees.

- **small-c.com –** a specialized service portal aimed at enabling independent consultants with services that include:
    - access to toll-free dialing and virtual assistant switchboards
    - access to temporary office services when required
    - training/certification in various tools, techniques and methodologies
    - access to remote meeting tools and common consulting tools like teleconference bridges
    - promotion and securing of mandates through our customer-facing portal - ExecutiveOutcomes

- **small-pm.com –** an ongoing project, this is our own, free/publicly available project management methodology for small to intermediate projects ranging from teams of 5-20 and durations from a few weeks to 6-8 months.

Also in the works is **small-smf** – the small serve management framework – designed to help IT organizations (and other service-delivery groups) standardize their service offerings and establish an integrated and management approach to delivering services to customers by starting with a common-sense right-sized ITIL approach.

We'll be looking forward to updating you in 2012 and beyond.